# WET PETS
## AND OTHER WATERY TALES

*A Collection of Short Stories*

# WET PETS
## AND OTHER WATERY TALES

*A Collection of Short Stories*

Edited by
HAZEL HITSON WEIDMAN
JACQUELINE KORONA TEARE

Printed in Victoria, Canada

**Note for Librarians:** a cataloguing record for this book that includes Dewey Classification and US Library of Congress numbers is available from the National Library of Canada. The complete cataloguing record can be obtained from the National Library's online database at: www.nlc-bnc.ca/amicus/index-e.html

ISBN 1-4120-1516-2

# TRAFFORD

**This book was published** *on-demand* **in cooperation with Trafford Publishing.** On-demand publishing is a unique process and service of making a book available for retail sale to the public taking advantage of on-demand manufacturing and Internet marketing. **On-demand publishing** includes promotions, retail sales, manufacturing, order fulfilment, accounting and collecting royalties on behalf of the author.

Suite 6E, 2333 Government St., Victoria, B.C. V8T 4P4, CANADA
Phone       250-383-6864       Toll-free   1-888-232-4444 (Canada & US)
Fax         250-383-6804       E-mail      sales@trafford.com
Web site    www.trafford.com   TRAFFORD PUBLISHING IS A DIVISION OF TRAFFORD HOLDINGS LTD.
Trafford Catalogue #03-1894    www.trafford.com/robots/03-1894.html

10       9       8       7       6       5       4       3

*For all those who care about animals*

**WET PETS**

# *Contents*

# *Foreword*

Books, dogs, and boats have been a holy trinity for me as long as I can remember. Very infrequently have these loves come together as they have in the pages of *Wet Pets*....

When I started *Maine Boats & Harbors* magazine in 1987, the first editorial department in place was "Boatyard Dog." Since the very beginning it has been a reader favorite.

The dog that inspired the column was Fagin, my Golden Retriever, a dog I got right after college and who soon joined me working the docks at the Henry R. Hinckley Company. I have never known a being more enthusiastic about going to work than Mr. F. He would dance on his hind legs, yelping for joy all the way down the long wharf every morning until he could jump aboard the yard boat *Roustabout*. His career, and mine, soon moved into publishing. First at *Wooden Boat* and then as we both became older dogs, at our own magazine. Books, boats, and dogs.

Out of the "Boatyard Dog" column grew a series of annual regattas, called "Goin' to the Dogs," that we held in Camden and Rockport Harbors. The first regatta was featured in the *Camden Herald*, along with a photo of our canine boat crews with a "No Dogs Allowed" sign in the background. The proceeds from these events went to the Camden-Rockport Animal Shelter.

It was soon after one of these regattas that the editors of *Wet Pets* ... came to the offices of *Maine Boats & Harbors* to discuss their project. I am so glad they persevered and did not let the mental

"No Dogs Allowed" sign dissuade them. The result is this fine book about boats and dogs (and a few cats, too).

John K. Hanson, Jr., Publisher
*Maine Boats & Harbors*
The Magazine of the Coast

Cats? Yes, indeed, and a couple of ducks, too.
*The Editors*

# *Introduction*

This book is a labor of love by two volunteers for the Camden-Rockport Animal Rescue League (CRARL) located in Rockport, Maine. It is a collection of stories written by people who are animal lovers at heart and whose pets have enriched their lives. The stories, no matter how short or how long, are loving tributes to cherished furry companions (or feathered friends) who have shared watery locations, waterborne adventures, or a special liking for water in environments where other features of terrain and climate may predominate.

The stories also represent a willingness to contribute time and effort to a project that will benefit those residents in our local, no-kill animal shelter who are awaiting adoption into homes that are as nurturing as those reflected in these tales. All proceeds from the sale of this book will go directly toward programs designed to enhance their well-being.

The stories were collected over a period of several years that must have seemed endless to our contributors. The authors stayed with us through all the trials and tribulations of a wholly volunteer project. E-mails and other correspondence went back and forth. Questions were asked and answered. Stories were sometimes expanded or rearranged or even slightly condensed, but approval of their final form rested with the authors.

Photographs were retrieved from storage boxes and albums and loaned to us to illustrate the unique character and appearance of the pets involved. Pictures of some were not available, but, through their owners' words, they have come to life in our imaginations.

Some of the pets described in this collection lived many years ago. Others are very much alive as we go to press. In several instances we received word of the death of a beloved companion whose personality and behavior had been affectionately described in a story. On these occasions we shared with our author friends their terrible sense of loss.

Now, we acknowledge how glad we are that the pets whose stories are included will become known and appreciated by others. By contributing to a worthwhile cause on behalf of stray, neglected, abused, and abandoned creatures, the authors of the stories have also contributed lasting memorials to their own unique companions. We thank them all.

The entire project has been a grand adventure, and we are pleased to offer this collection for your enjoyment.

# Behind the Cover Photo

Four years ago Rod Choate found Sadie, a "full-blooded Water Beagle pup," living on the edge of the Cobbossee Stream in West Gardiner, Maine, and adopted her.

She loves to ride in the car but often gets car sick, reports the South Gardiner man. "But the high seas don't bother her a bit. She has been out in four- or five-foot swells and loves every minute of it."

The Choates now take her everywhere they go in their boat—to the lake, down the river, to the open ocean. She loves it all. Her spot is the bow of the boat. "Bow Wow Rider," she's always on the lookout for seagulls, seals, and cormorants. Nothing escapes her sharp eye.

In the cover photo, the Choate vessel is doing about 15 knots, approaching Fort Popham on the Kennebec River. Choate says this is the speed at which "the ears begin to develop lift and fly on their own."

Our thanks to Rod Choate and Sadie for the perfect photo to open this collection of "Wet Pet" tales.

*The Editors*

*Sadie at her post*

## LADY CAMPBELL—"BEST DOG"

≋

### By Jane H. Scarpino
#### Port Clyde, Maine

Awhile back, looking through some old albums, searching for a picture of an old friend, I came across a faded snapshot of a Boston Terrier. Printed underneath, in childish hand: "The best dog in the world."

It took me back fifty years! Old friend, indeed. It was our Lady Campbell. Ah ... the memories.

We first saw her when her young master, commanding the USCG Cutter *Campbell*, was on leave visiting his parents. (Our families had been friends, and we grew up together.) He had bought the pup for company on the long voyages across the North Atlantic, where the *Campbell* was on convoy duty. He gave her the ship's name, and she was "good luck" mascot for the crew. And this is why.

They saw a lot of action. During one attack, they rammed an enemy submarine and had to abandon ship. In the confusion, the dog was overlooked. Seamen are a superstitious lot, and as they sat in the lifeboats watching their ship wallowing in the swells, they must have wondered about their luck. But the *Campbell* did not sink, and they boarded her again, to find—still swimming around in the hold—Lady Campbell.

She was four years old when the war was over. Her master was reassigned to Alaska, and could not take her with him. So, Lady Campbell came to us, in her little navy blue coat with the red trim, a small anchor emblazoned on the stern end. She had finally come ashore.

The family was delighted to have her; she was good company for us all, but it soon became obvious that her new master, her love, was our eight-year-old son Jon. She slept with him and shadowed him wherever he went. They were inseparable, except when he was in school, and then she would wait for the bus to bring him home. My mind sees them still, walking to the pond, fishing pole over Jon's shoulder, Cam at his heels. She had the utmost patience and a lot of curiosity about fishing.

Bulldogs are notorious snorers, and our Cam was no exception. After a few nights, we had all adjusted. It was just a kind of comforting night sound, but at one point, my neighbors thought I was keeping another man while my husband was at sea!

One winter's night, amidst a howling snowstorm, there was a smoky fire in the cellar of our house (spontaneous combustion in an old grass rug). The kids were all just getting over bad colds, and I didn't want to take them out if it wasn't necessary. The firemen agreed to let us stay as long as it

*Lady Campbell— "Best dog" —with the author's daughter Karin*

was safe; so we opened all the windows, settled the children, wrapped in blankets, on the couch, while a little smoke wafted around them. Lady Campbell huddled close to Jon—but no one was frightened. Suddenly, black smoke billowed from the old registers like an acrid fog, and two policemen with flashlights appeared.

"Time to go!" they said, picked up the kids, threw blankets over their heads, and started off.

"Where's my dog?" I asked, not able to see her in the smoke, and surely not wanting to leave her behind.

"Right behind you, Lady," answered the men, and we made our way out to a neighbor's house.

When the fire was out and it was safe to return, except for no heat, I left the children with my neighbors and returned to my own bed. Cam came with me, shivering and shaking with fear and cold, but determined. Together we huddled under the covers until morning.

She always had a thing about water, probably from her days of enemy action. One time, an unsuspecting neighbor was watering his lawn, when a small black and white fury attacked the hose in his hand, wresting it away, shaking it, snapping and snarling, and thoroughly soaking him!

When we swam, I had to shut her away. At the sight of us in the water, she was beside herself, jumping in, and trying to herd us all back to dry land and safety. On the other side of the coin, she loved the boats, often curling up in the sun on the stern seat of the rowboat. When they attached the motor, she rode in the bow, head up, like a small bowsprit!

One day, several young families and neighbors were at the beach. It was a bit cold, and the kids were building sand castles, the dog an interested spectator. She really thought she was a kid! The parents stood in knee-deep water, just talking. A five-year-old was one of the group of children and had been sternly told NOT to go into the water. To be safe, his Mom had put a life jacket on him. However, warnings don't mean much to five-year-olds and it wasn't long before he was close to venturing in—not his mother, nor anyone else noticing.

A sudden commotion on the beach made us all turn around. Children were yelling, and Cam was dashing, barking madly, down the beach and into the water, towards a small object bobbing face down, his orange jacket holding him that way. He had stumbled and lost his balance, and could have drowned at the back of his mother's knee had it not been for Lady Campbell!

One night when Jon was away, she quietly pulled her bed over behind a chair, and went to sleep. The silence was deafening, and woke us up. We buried her in the morning with tears, and the boys made her a wooden cross that read: "Lady Campbell, the best dog in the world."

Years have gone by; we have loved other pets, but she remains in our hearts. Always a lady, her heart and courage as large as the men's she sailed with on her namesake, the USCG Cutter *Campbell*.

≈≈≈

Jane Scarpino is author of the popular children's book, *Nellie the Lighthouse Dog*. She lives in the one-hundred-and-fifty-year-old home in Port Clyde, Maine, which she and her late husband, Captain H.C. (Skip) Scarpino, bought when they retired in 1980. The Scarpinos were charter members of the area's Marshall Point (lighthouse) Restoration Committee, and Jane still opens and closes the lighthouse during the summer months. Mother of four, she is now grandmother to three girls, and, as of this writing, has three Boston Terriers "who are loving and entertaining and keep me warm in bed at night—but really, there has never been another Lady Campbell." Inspired by the writing of Cam's story, she recently reconnected with the dog's original owner, the young commander of the USCG Cutter *Campbell*—now retired Vice Admiral Austin Wagner.

# MEG—A SMALL BUT MIGHTY SWIMMER

≈≈≈

## By Townsend Hornor
### Osterville, Massachusetts

For a number of years I have run a very small marine service business in Osterville on Cape Cod. I have also had a life-long love affair with dogs, and for a time raised Labrador Retrievers. More recently, reflecting the restrictions of a pickup truck cab and a small, open, half-decked work boat, I switched to West Highland Whites. Surprising to some, I've found these dogs demonstrate many of the Labrador attributes of loyalty and companionship, spunk, and love of the water—albeit usually the fore shore rather than anything much deeper. And, they are a better size for me.

One day about eight years ago, I was out with an associate looking for a client's mooring that needed a new pennant. We were accompanied by a rather small year-old Westie bitch named Meg, who weighed perhaps eight or nine pounds and, when swimming, floated with her small head barely visible in the water. You guessed it: she fell overboard, unseen! I am usually very careful to keep an eye on whatever dog I have with me, as he or she may roam around the narrow side decks of my work boat; but this time I goofed as I concentrated on searching for the missing mooring.

It was blowing northwest 15-20 mph and cool for a spring day. We were in a bay about a quarter mile from the nearest shore on either side of us. We looked and looked, more and more frantically, but after almost an hour we finally gave up. I returned home, telling my good wife that I had carelessly drowned our youngest dog. I sat down in despair. What was there to say?

About thirty minutes later, the telephone rang. A friend asked if we were missing one of our Westies! The dog had swum the quarter mile to shore in the choppy water, climbed up on the marsh bank, then traveled another quarter mile to our friend's house. When I arrived, Meg was playing vigorously with one of his dogs, liberally coated with marsh mud on her belly!

Cats may have nine lives. Meg has at least that number and an incredible amount of spunk and muscle and energy, too. She is now nine, has played Toto in the *Wizard of Oz* with a local theater group, and is looking for new worlds to conquer. And, when the water is warmer, she swims!

*Spunky Meg—water lover and survivor*

≈≈

Townsend Hornor wrote Meg's story in late 1998, one of the very first contributed to this volume. He lives on Cape Cod in a waterfront house his father bought in 1927. As of 2003 he and his wife had two dogs: Molly, a rescued Cocker Spaniel, and Sheba, a Golden Retriever/Shepherd mix. Following a career in investment banking, "Townie" (as he is often called) opened a small-boat service business in Osterville. He is currently Chairman of the National Marine Life Center, which is working to build a rehabilitation facility along the Cape Cod Canal in Buzzards Bay for stranded marine mammals. He is, or has been, active in a number of other charitable institutions on and around the Cape.

# PILOT OF THE *TIMBERWIND*

≋

## *By Capt. Rick Miles*
*Schooner* Timberwind
*Rockport, Maine*

Yes, Pilot is a water dog. She has been my constant friend and companion for almost seven years now. When thoughts of spring begin to come around again, and I begin to think about preparing the schooner for the sailing season, I try to remember my life aboard ship without Pilot—and I can't. You see, her course and mine crossed when I was a struggling new owner of a large sailing ship and she was a six-week-old pup—small enough to fit into my old steel-toed work boot. Back then I was living alone in the workshop with no heat or plumbing, and I figured it was about time that I got that dog I had always wanted. Next thing I knew, there she was. It was the beginning of a fast and true friendship.

*Pilot in a pensive mood*

The following summer Pilot sailed with me on every trip aboard the *Timberwind*, taking folks from all over sailing along the beautiful coast of Maine. Pilot took right to the water, partly because she is a black Labrador Retriever, but mostly because we just wanted to be together, and I happened to spend half of the year living and sailing on my schooner.

That black dog really enjoys sailing on the *Timberwind*, and the folks who sail with us love her. Why, some come back year after year just to see Pilot. Well, spring is not too far away and here in Rockport, Maine, there are a man and his dog whose eyes are beginning to look back out to the bay.

*Life is good with a special treat now and then*

Pilot is quite at home on the *Timberwind*, in the yawl boat or in any vessel small or large, as long as I am with her. Sometimes when I'm running folks ashore in the yawl boat, I have to leave Pilot aboard the schooner. She never takes her eyes off of me the whole time. As I approach the schooner, even from a long way off, I can see her with her front paws hanging over the rail. When she thinks I am close enough to hear her, she yelps a bit. As I circle the schooner, she sprints from bow to stern, trying to keep an eye on me. She is vigilant, indeed.

About now, people might be wondering, "Where does Pilot do her 'business' while out on four-day trips aboard the *Timberwind*?" Well, twice each day she hops into the dory with me, and we row ashore. Just as the bow eases up on the beach she jumps out and does what she has to do—below the high tide line, of course.

Resting in the shade under the big main boom has become her favorite spot for presiding over the ship's company each day. She's so good at it she can do it with her eyes closed, with an occasional snore just to let everyone think that she's not watching.

Pilot is famous around the fleet, and few vessels sail by without calling to her. That dog of mine responds each and every time with a big loud, "ship ahoy." At least, that's how I translate it. Then, on the last day of the trip Pilot stands watch as we enter Rockport Harbor. She is always the first one off the vessel. She is greeted by her adopted Labrador-sister Maggie, my wife Karen, and harbormaster Leroy Dodge. She has a big smile and tail wag for each of them.

This was written by me, Capt. Rick Miles, in the year 2000, on a windy, snowy day here on Pleasant Mountain in West Rockport, Maine. Pilot is curled up on her rug in front of the wood stove, dreaming, no doubt, about the next warm season on the water.

~~~

After owning and operating the pilot schooner *Timberwind* for twelve years, Capt. Rick and his wife Capt. Karen (author of the *Remarkable Maggie* story next in this volume) now own and operate the Expedition Vessel *Wanderbird*. They do nature-themed cruises along the coasts of Maine, Nova Scotia, and the province of Newfoundland and Labrador. Website www.wanderbirdcruises.com provides additional information about them and their new adventure.

# REMARKABLE MAGGIE

≋

## By Capt. Karen Miles
### Rockport, Maine

Maggie, a two-year-old black Labrador Retriever mix, is my constant companion and work mate. Maggie and I work on my dad's lobster boat. Each morning at 5 a.m. we pack our lunches (sandwiches and doggie kibble) and head for the harbor. Maggie loves to ride in boats. She is always ready to charge down the gangway and jump aboard for another day's adventure.

We row a tiny skiff out to the mooring and climb aboard. I tap the rail of the lobster boat and Maggie jumps three feet up from the skiff to scramble aboard. She then proceeds to do a complete circle around the rails and bow to make sure everything is in order.

We head for the pier where we purchase our fuel and sell lobsters. If Billy, the lobster buyer, is around, Mag jumps off the boat to greet him. He usually has a head-pat for Maggie, and sometimes even a biscuit.

As we steam out on the bay for our long day's work, Maggie takes in a good dose of salt air, her ears blowing in the breeze. Once the rhythm of the day has been established, she curls up on the engine box where it is always warm—even on the coldest days.

Maggie's tasks aboard this working vessel are: alerting us to runaway lobsters, badgering feisty crabs, warning errant gulls away from the bait bin, guarding lunch, and keeping both my father and me within ears length. From Mag's perspective, a good day's catch amounts to several "extra" lobster legs left in the saltwater tank after all of the day's catch has been removed and crated. These delicious tidbits are her favorite snacks.

At the end of each day, we all are dog-tired. On my voice command, Mag carefully jumps down out of the lobster boat into the tiny skiff, and we row ashore as the sun sets. Maggie is a truly brave and amazing dog. This goes unnoticed by most people. You see, the remarkable thing about Maggie is that she has been blind since birth.

*Remarkable Maggie— "seeing" through her ears*

P.S. Maggie is the loving, adopted sister to Pilot of the *Timberwind*.

Capt. Karen Miles, wife of Capt. Rick Miles (author of the preceding *Pilot* story), is a licensed ship captain with many artistic talents. She submitted no biographical information, preferring to focus on Maggie's story. But we are happy to report that black Labs Pilot and Maggie both live aboard the Miles' new Expedition Vessel *Wanderbird*—along with a parrot and a finch. Further information is available on their Website: www.wanderbirdcruises.com.

# WON TON KITTY

≈

## By *Alicia E. Albright*
### *Washington, Maine*

While growing up on a farm in rural Maine, it wasn't unusual to have any number of stray cats show up to keep warm and be fed in our barn. We had so many strays over the years, it became obvious our farm had become a drop-off for unwanted pets. But that wasn't always to our disadvantage. Many a stray proved his or her worth over time through pest control, companionship, or even just a really loud purr to do the chores by. I guess it wasn't too surprising when one of those strays, who became near and dear to our hearts, proved he may have been as crafty as a cat, but also as loyal as a dog.

When Won Ton showed up, he was a straggly, dirty, skin-and-bones wreck of a cat. He was already mostly grown. It was obvious from the start that he had a bold spirit. Maybe that's how he got his name. I don't remember how we came up with it, exactly. But, you know the hero dog of cartoon fame, Hong Kong Phooey? Well, we had Won Ton Kitty. Once Won Ton was in residence, he set out to make sure that he never got evicted. He showed an immediate affinity for my sister Missy and became "her" cat within days.

But that wasn't enough for Won Ton. I believe he got it into his head that everybody was going to love him.

He started following us wherever we went. Walk out the door, and he was at your feet. Out to get the mail, Won Ton trailed you. You couldn't shake that cat. Maybe he figured if he never let us out of his sight, he would be as close to his food source as any cat could be. I prefer to think that Won Ton was just loyal. And it was this devoted nature that eventually led us to discover we had quite a unique kitty on our hands. He's the only one I've ever heard of and certainly the only

one I've ever had the privilege of personally knowing.

*Won Ton Kitty — fascinated by all of the activity in the fish tank*

Of course, living in the country with a cat-who-won't-be-left-behind can be an inconvenience, especially if you want to scout the woods for deer during hunting season. When that cat followed my parents out hunting one day, they decided to cut him off at the pass. "Let's cross over the stream, here, where it's deep," suggested my mother, "so we can leave the cat behind." Then Ma and Dad jumped the rocks to get to the other side. But Won Ton was not to be deterred, even by a flowing stream. That crazy kitty didn't even try to jump the stones. He dove right in and started swimming. Yup, that cat could SWIM! He wasn't just flailing around, either. He was a good, strong swimmer, who wouldn't be left behind! My parents couldn't believe their eyes, and laughed until they almost cried.

Of course we all heard about it, and most of us even had the opportunity to see Won Ton in action. Swimming seemed to be second nature to him. He swam whenever he got the chance. Was Won Ton just a dog at heart? I can't say for sure, but I choose to believe that he was a cat that would go to any lengths to remain by our sides.

I know cats are supposed to be afraid of the water, and maybe most cats are, but Won Ton was our amazing swimming kitty who filled our days with laughter and tales to tell during the few short years that he lived with us. Sadly, just as suddenly as he showed up in our barn, he disappeared one day. Maybe the swashbuckler swam away to greater adventures. More likely he is no longer alive, but perhaps more importantly, he remains alive and vivid in our memories—a champion cat among dozens of barn drop-offs.

He could have been just one of the many meowing minions, but instead, took his place in Pepler pets' history as Won Ton Kitty—Swimming Cat *Extraordinaire*.

〰〰

Alicia E. (Pepler) Albright was born Alicia Elaine Dale in Providence, R.I., on December 10, 1968. After her father died of cancer, her mother remarried, and the newly formed Pepler family moved to Realm Farm, in Liberty, Maine. There they raised goats, chickens, cows, horses and many cats and dogs. After graduating from Mt. View High School, Alicia earned a bachelor's degree in speech communication, with highest honors, from the University of Maine. She married David F. Albright, MCSE, in 1990 and is the mother of three: Alic, Dashiell, and LiLi. The Albright pets are Willow and Shilo, neutered Siamese cats, and Lila, a neutered part-Bernese Mountain Dog and shelter rescue. The antics of her animals continue to amaze and inspire her. She recently earned her master's degree in education and hopes to teach elementary school children.

## GEORGE—THE ALMOST-PERFECT DOG

≋

*By Jen Lothrop*
*Rockland, Maine*

This story is about my dog named George.

George is a mixed breed, 10 percent Alsatian, which is like a German Shepherd, and 90 percent black Lab. He came to us as a stray, abused dog. We decided to give him a ten-day trial run to see whether or not we would keep him. He made it. Since that time he has made a big difference in our lives.

George's name has a story. My family and I were writing down names to draw out of a hat. I was in my brother's room reading off the names of the presidents list-ed in a book. I would read all the last names first and then the first names. My mom and dad were in their room and heard me read out "George" from George Washington. My parents loved it. That's how we came up with the name George.

I can talk to George when no one else is around. I practiced my pet first aid

*George*

on George when I was taking Home Economics in the sixth grade. George isn't finicky about food. He eats anything and everything except pickles and onions. He also makes the whole family cheery, because after his dinner every night he goes to the living room, scratches his paws on the rug, lies down and rubs his face on the rug to get his face clean. This is not so good for the rug, but George is special.

George and I like to play ball, go for walks, and swim. He has a great interest in sleeping on my bed and a love of chewing/sucking on his deflated basketball. This ball enters into play with my dad, too. He will take George's ball and hide it under his arm while the dog tries to find it.

I have been interested in dogs for a long time. I have always wanted to be a dog trainer and one of those people who walk the dogs around in dog shows. I have never met a dog trainer, but I have read a lot of books about it. So I taught George new techniques like, "lie on your back," "sit," "paw," "fetch," and "shake" to use after he has been in the water or had a bath. My interest in training and my efforts to train George really paid off the day he went after a lobster buoy and would not come back when called.

One April day my mother and I took George swimming in the ocean. We were throwing sticks in the water for George to fetch. Well, he caught something all right. He caught a lobster buoy. My mom and I were calling him to come in, but while we were yelling, he was sinking. He could not pull the buoy in, but he wouldn't let go of it.

My mother thought the buoy might be caught in his mouth; so when she saw a person in a boat, she called out to him and pointed toward George. This man's common sense told him what had happened. He offered to take my mom out in the boat to see if the buoy really was caught in the George's mouth. They were not sure that George could get into the boat from the water, so my mom just pulled on his collar and grabbed the buoy. The buoy came out of his mouth into my mom's hand, and it was so slimy it fell into the water again.

Since they knew the buoy was not caught in George's mouth, the two of them came back to the dock. But George still wouldn't leave the buoy. My mother called to him again, but he would not come. Then I really shouted at him to get himself back to shore NOW. Only then did he come in on his own. He knew I meant it. I think the time that I had spent training George made the difference. I would like to think so, anyway.

George's one bad habit is that he sometimes gets into the trash. Maybe if I learn more about dog training, I will be able to teach him not to do that. I guess I could make that my next training project. George is such a wonderful dog it just might make him perfect!

≋

*Almost-perfect-dog George with the author*

Jennifer Lothrop (who prefers to be called "Jen") was twelve years old when this was written. She lives in Rockland, Maine, and hopes one day to become an eye doctor. Her hobbies include swimming, playing with her black Lab George and being with friends. Her favorite song is "Graduation" by Vitamin C, and her favorite color is green. Jennifer has an older brother Michael. In the summer of 2001, Jennifer was one of eight Rockland-area teens honored for volunteer work through Youthlinks, a nonprofit community service group.

# SPOOKY'S ADVENTURE

≋

## *By Roger F. Duncan, East Boothbay, Maine, and Betty Roberts, Friendship, Maine*

Spooky was a black cat that sailed with the Swanson Family aboard their Friendship Sloop, the *Jolly Buccaneer*. Spooky, whose undetermined sex we shall identify as female, was the central figure involved in a little side trip on the Friendship Sloop *Eastward*, which was moored near the *Jolly Buccaneer*. The adventure began the night of the banquet held to celebrate the end of the 1964 Friendship Sloop Regatta in Friendship, Maine.

The races were over, and the sloops were at anchor in Friendship Harbor. The awards had been given out after the banquet in town, where there had been much camaraderie along with the good food— but no drinks, because Friendship was a dry town. When people returned to their sloops after the banquet, the owner of the *Eastward* found his boat nudging up against the *Jolly Buccaneer*. They were swung apart so they wouldn't bump into each other during the night.

But as owner Roger Duncan was rowing his party back to the *Eastward* and they were approaching the sloop, his wife Mary said she thought she saw a cat go aboard. No one else had seen anything, but just to be sure, the crew of the *Eastward* searched the vessel; no cat. They called for it to come to them; no cat. They brought out sardines and milk, but no cat emerged. As it seemed increasingly evident to those involved in the search that there was no cat aboard, Mary Duncan began to be teased about "seeing things." "Oh, sure, cat on board!" "Perhaps one too many drinks during the evening's festivities?"

Mary Duncan never fell prey to the seduction of alcoholic beverages, but this night she bore the brunt of much laughter and talk about drinks, visions, hallucinations, etc. With all the laughter and joking, word soon got around the wharf that the *Eastward* had a phantom cat aboard.

Finally, the search and the merriment ended. People quieted down for the night, and the next morning the *Eastward* sailed for Newagen, her home port near Boothbay. As they shoved off, Roger Duncan announced (with tongue-in-cheek) to others on the wharf, that if anyone had lost a cat, it could be found aboard his ship when he tied up in Newagen.

Shortly after the *Eastward* departed, a tearful Swanson girl appeared on the wharf asking if anyone had seen her black cat, whose name was "Spooky." She was told that Spooky was OK and on the way to Newagen aboard the *Eastward*. Her smile was radiant, and the happy youngster raced to her father's boat, the *Jolly Buccaneer*, to let her family know that Spooky was aboard the *Eastward*.

When the *Eastward* arrived at its home port, the Swanson girl was on the dock, asking about her pet. The Duncans checked all around again, looking for the cat but found none. Then, the Swanson girl called Spooky by name. Out she came. She had been there all along, but wouldn't reveal herself to anyone except her little mistress or some other person with a well-recognized voice.

Apparently the *Jolly Buccaneer* and the *Eastward* were moored close enough together the night before, that when they nuzzled together Spooky could cross from one sloop to the other. She must have decided to investigate the *Eastward*, but before she could return, the vessels were separated. There was no way to get back home, and she ended up in Newagen the next day. What a relief it must have been to hear her mistress' voice in the midst of all the strangeness about her.

Needless to say, Mary Duncan's statement about a cat being aboard was vindicated. And there was great rejoicing when Spooky was finally back home aboard the *Jolly Buccaneer* after her unintended adventure. Her story still brings smiles and comments from those who remember her and this incident, which ended so happily.

≋

At the time of this happening in Friendship, Roger Duncan was a teacher and Assistant Headmaster at Belmont Hill School in Belmont, Massachusetts. During the summers he and his wife sailed parties in their Friendship sloop *Eastward* from Newagen, Maine. They took time off this particular week to race with other Friendship sloops in the annual Homecoming Regatta in Friendship. Since then, he has spent a year as Headmaster, retired from teaching, and moved year-round to East Boothbay, Maine. He and his wife have given up the sloop and now sail a small schooner, *Dorothy Elizabeth*, and write articles and an occasional book. For more than twenty years Roger Duncan has been Yearbook Editor for the Friendship Sloop Society.

≋

At the time of Spooky's adventure, Elizabeth Roberts and her husband owned and operated a lobster wharf in Friendship Harbor. They bought lobsters from the fishermen and sold them wholesale. She suspects that the enticing odors of fish and lobsters permeating the wooden surface of the wharf may have lured Spooky in that direction via the *Eastward*. Betty, as she is known locally and to members of the Friendship Sloop Society, has for many years functioned in different capacities as an officer of the Society. As of this writing she is serving as Historian.

## DUFFY—WITH SHEBA TO THE RESCUE

≋

*By Jae Pillsbury*
*South Thomaston, Maine*

High on a hill, surrounded by woods and fields along the estuary of the Weskeag River in South Thomaston, Maine, live MacDuff and his mom. MacDuff is a West Highland Terrier that many will recognize as one of those adorable little dogs bred to be small-animal hunters on the moors in Scotland. Whether digging, chasing, or waiting patiently, the breed is noted for its tenacity, and MacDuff is true to his breed.

When he was a pup, "Duffy," as he is called, would roam far and wide on the land, exploring fox holes, rolling in wonderful smells, and eating seaweed that had washed onto the mud flats at low tide. He also loved to swim. But his very favorite thing was treeing squirrels. When he was successful at that, he would sit under the tree where his quarry was hiding and just watch. He didn't care about anything else. With the tenacity built into him, he would stay there all day, even in danger-ously cold or stormy weather. His mom would call and call, but he wouldn't "come." He would "give her a woof" when she asked him to. Then she could tell where he was, and, if necessary, go and rescue him.

As the years have passed, things have changed. Duffy and his mom have gotten old and lame, and the squirrels have almost disappeared. For exercise now, this devoted pair just takes long walks.

In snowy weather they use the long lane that is their driveway. Often they stop and visit with a neighbor, Donna, and her Border Collie Sheba. Duff and Sheba have good times together and sometimes Sheba, who is much younger than Duffy, will come up the hill all by herself for a friendly visit. She has nice long legs and can run effort-lessly through tall grass and snow, but she also goes right home when Donna calls. She is not as addicted to squirrels as MacDuff!

One day last winter, following a series of heavy snows, Duffy was walking off-leash along the driveway with his mom, when he smelled or heard a SQUIRREL. In spite of deep snow and arthritically old, short legs, he couldn't resist the call—off he went across the field into the woods. His mom called and called, but he wouldn't "come." She was frantic, imagining all sorts of misfortune that might befall him. He could be stuck in the deep snow—in too much pain to struggle free. He might have become disoriented in all the whiteness. There are predators in the Maine woods. He might be in serious danger. She might never recover him.

*Rescuer Sheba in summer sunshine*

Mom didn't dare try to go to him, because she is old and arthritic, too. She went back up the driveway to the top of the hill and, from the deck of their house, she asked Duffy to "give her a woof." He did. She could just barely see him far off in the deep snow. He was sitting —or was he stuck? What to do?

Then mom had an idea. Maybe if Duffy thought Sheba were nearby or at the house, he would try to come see her; so she called out Sheba's name. About a half-mile away Sheba heard and came running up the lane. When she got to the place where Duffy had taken off, she instinctively turned and followed his trail. Watching from the deck mom could see that Sheba had found

*Duffy rests after his squirrel watch*

him. Distracting him from his squirrel-watch, Sheba managed to get Duffy to play with her. Then she led him out to the lane. Sheba ran ahead up the hill to tell Duffy's mom that all was well. And by the time the tired, lame, old squirrel-hunter got home, winter coat soaking wet from snow deeper than he is tall, Sheba and Duffy's mom were having treats together. Duffy, of course, got some, too.

≋

JoAnne E. Pillsbury, or "Jae," as she prefers to be called, grew up in Wellesley Hills, Massachusetts, graduated from Middlebury College in Vermont, and worked for a time as a cancer researcher at Massachusetts General Hospital. After her marriage she continued her research while her naval officer husband served in Vietnam. When he returned, she became a stay-at-home mother to their two children until they were both in school. She then taught secondary school math while her husband worked in the family business in Massachusetts. During this time, the Pillsburys summered in Maine and, upon retirement, built a home in South Thomaston. "Duff and I are alone now since Peter died, but we are very fortunate to live in such a special place."

# TIGGER AND POOH—TRIMARAN TRAVELERS

## By Rosemary Anderson
### Port Townsend, Washington

My husband and I built a 30-foot Piver Trimaran and sailed it to Florida. Our two cats, Tigger and Pooh, came along. All in all they seemed very content with life on the boat. It helped to have the extra deck space of a trimaran. While on board, however, they did use up some of their equity in nine lives.

On separate occasions each cat fell overboard and survived. Contrary to what people believe, cats can swim very well—if not by choice. They didn't have to swim far, though. Each time one fell into the water, he managed to climb up the sheer fiberglass side of the hull to safety. Also, each seemed

*Tigger at home on the water*

to have learned a lesson from the experience, because these were one-time events for both cats.

These episodes alone were frightening, but our greatest challenge came one day while we were having trouble with our engine as we motored into Saybrook, Connecticut. Fumes were sinking into the main cabin, but we didn't realize it until I went below and found both cats—overcome. I quickly carried them up on deck, gave them mouth-to-mouth resuscitation and tried to walk them around. Luckily, those efforts paid off. Both recovered completely.

I often wonder if anyone on shore was watching that peculiar sight!

Tigger and Pooh, our good sailing buddies, are no longer with us, but we remember them and our sea-faring adventures together, with warmth and humor.

*Pooh—checking out the rigging*

Rosemary Anderson grew up in Scotland, completed college, then came to the United States to work as a governess. She met and married husband Andy, with whom she has shared thirty memorable years. They were living in Massachusetts in the '70s, when they began to build their trimaran. While doing so, they built and spent a year in a small cabin in the woods—cramped quarters, no electricity or running water, but, as she says, "good preparation for life on board." They sailed to Florida and lived aboard with Tigger and Pooh, eventually selling the boat and buying land on which they built a house in Tampa. They returned to Massachusetts in 1985 and built the house in which they lived at the time this story was contributed (1999). In 2002 they moved back to Rosemary's roots in Scotland but returned to the United States in 2003 and promptly bought a sailboat, about which Rosemary comments: "Here we go again!"

The Andersons have three children. Shana has followed in her parents' footsteps, has her own business, and is a builder of classic wooden boats in Port Townsend, Washington. David has an interest in film and has had parts as an extra in several movies in Hollywood, California. Victoria, a high school student, is interested in photography and marine biology. Cats have always been an important part of their family but they are "in-between" pets as this goes to press.

# Chester—Famous Sailing Dog

## By Dorrie Long
### Camden, Maine

It isn't easy having a famous dog. People recognize him but not us. His fame is due to his obeying the only command I have successfully taught him, one which most dogs and their owners would never imagine.

Put him on a sailboat and tell him "Go on"—up goes his leg at the rail and over the side it whizzes. People ashore and on other boats have been known to point, cheer, applaud, laugh, and, my personal favorites, whistle and bark. He is, after all, a very large Chesapeake Bay Retriever on a boat! Sailing dog-owners quite often stare in fascinated admiration.

We have been judging his performance for years, using the ice-skating scoring system. The 10's have predominated, even in this his tenth summer. And for those who wonder about the other necessities of life on board, just know that a dustpan situated in a convenient spot

*Chester — beloved sailing companion*

on deck allows transfers into the holding tank with no problems whatsoever.

Chester was the first dog to sail in the Caribbean 1500 (through a Force 9 Gale), and he has sailed to Bermuda, the Bahamas, the Turks and Caicos, the Virgin Islands, up the Intracoastal Waterway and, of course, along the coast of Maine, performing and becoming famous. Not bad for a pet shop puppy we saved from an animal shelter in Massachusetts where he had been left because he was too big and bouncy!

*Famous Chester*

Dorrie Long and her husband have sailed with Chester from Maine to the Caribbean. While cruising the Chesapeake Bay, Dorrie was horrified to have Chester identified as a Weimaraner. Recently, they have been joined by Samantha, a Schipperke, who frequently becomes seasick and, according to Dorrie's husband, hates everyone but her mistress.

# BUSTER—BEST OF THE BELFAST STRAYS

## By Lynda Clancy
### Rockport, Maine

B elfast has its share of characters, many of whom are the foundation for a small Maine city renowned for its creativity and vibrant eccentricity. It is a community of humans and animals who do not cave in to mediocrity. Where else do you find a city peppered with cats that look more like bulldogs?

But the Belfast character who trotted into our lives with such humor and sweetness was neither human nor feline; he was a dog—and mind you, no ordinary dog. He was a Belfast stray.

Back in 1989, Buster spent some time at Fitzjurls' Townline Animal Shelter after he was found grazing in the garbage behind the Opera House. Then he moved into our home and hearts.

*Dominic Dill, Buster's very good friend and Lynda's son, gives his pal the best kind of hug only a five-year-old boy can give a dog*

He was a dog of incredible strength, a mixture of black Labrador Retriever, Newfoundland, and Chow, or so surmised Dr. George Holmes, who based his opinion on the black spots on Buster's tongue. You could also tell by Buster's stance that his breed once really did guard the castle. No bark was ever so deep and ferocious; no dog so utterly benign.

And his hearing remains unsurpassed by any creature I've known. He knew when he arrived that his place was several notches below Egypt, the ancient cat, and that Maggie, our Belgian Shepherd, was alpha dog. But there was no need to train him; he was way above us with his sensitivity and intelligence.

Eventually, he established that he was a person, and as our two baby boys flowered into toddler-hood, Buster refused to ride in the far back of the station-wagon like a mere dog. His place was between the two small car seats. From there he could lean over and land a big lick on either baby's cheek, bringing squeals of joy from the back seat. If the boys happened not to be in the car with us, Buster took up occupancy in one of their car seats, squeezing his rump into the confines of babyhood, positioning himself to better survey the world with his head hung out the window.

And, try as I might to convince him that his daily visits around the neighborhood might bring out the dogcatcher, Buster stuck to his ways. Who were we to regulate his lifestyle? If there were rounds to make, Buster was going to make them—even if it meant his people had to wait until midnight to open the door when he trotted down the driveway.

After all the other animals and babies were bedded down, the door would open (husband Jim was awfully good about getting up to let Buster in), and Buster would trot in, bounce up onto the bed, curl up, and pass out.

His strength and spirit and smarts, I'm positive, grew from an early life on the streets. This was no kennel dog. When he was run over—literally—by a large Chevy truck in front of Key Bank in Belfast, did he lie on the ground? Heck no. He jumped up, and despite a broken hip, continued to run after his three-legged dog-friend Rambo, another stray who had found a home with a friend of ours. Whereas Buster had the enthusiasm and unrelenting warmth of a puppy, Rambo exuded the dignity of a crossbreed whose roots extended back to the wolf. Buster would cavort around Rambo, and Rambo would nail him with a swat—they truly loved each other. The broken hip? Merely a blip in Buster's otherwise zestful life.

His favorite spot was aboard our Boston Whaler, which Jim named after Buster. As Jim polished the teak on that Whaler, the sign-maker penned in perfect script on the transom, *Buster Boat*. It made perfect sense, once you knew Buster.

Our other dog, the Belgian Shepherd, had nothing but disdain for the water. Buster, on the other hand, would stand tall on the bow. With a 90-horsepower engine, across Penobscot Bay we'd fly, with the force of the wind pinning Buster's ears back and curling his snout into a ferocious snarl. So joyful; so alive.

That was the way of Buster, for the nearly nine too-short years he spent with us. Serene throughout his battle against cancer and until the night he died—serene even while death took him away. We know he's somewhere in the great living room of heaven—on a couch—resting up, waiting for us.

Lynda Clancy is a reporter and writer who lives in Rockport at the mercy of her menagerie, which includes two big dogs, a rabbit, an ancient cat, and, of course, her husband Jim Dill and sons Dominic and Lucas.

# TI-TI—THE FISHING CAT

≈≈≈

### By Kathy Bartlett
*Rockland, Maine*

As a former lakefront resident, I'd like to share the story of Ti-Ti (pronounced "Tie-Tie"), our fishing cat. Ti is no longer with us, but memories of his antics remain alive.

*Ti-Ti, fish in mouth, brings home the day's catch to share with his siblings*

We had Ti from infancy and suspect that his interest in water sports developed gradually—as he learned to connect our fishing trips with fishy suppers.

At the end of a day of fishing we could count on Ti-Ti to be waiting for the catch of the day, which he promptly and proudly carried up the wharf to generously share with his less sports-minded brothers.

He also did a bit of fishing on his own—curious, as most cats dislike water. He would wade into the shallows in front of our cottage and try to catch the plentiful but fast-moving minnows there. In spite of all of Ti's batting and swatting, the tiny fishes remained relatively unscathed.

We still have one of Ti's heirs, Benny, who seems to have inherited his love of water. Although Benny is strictly an inside cat, he thoroughly enjoys standing in and splashing around in his water dish.

*Ti-Ti's heir, Benny—Could it be the genes?*

≋

Kathy Bartlett is a Rockland native, recently retired from working part-time in the escort department at Penobscot Bay Medical Center. She and her husband are owned and loved by two cats, Benny and Bubbles, who are both nearing voting age. Kathy enjoys gardening, reading, writing, sewing, and crafts. She knits, too, but much to her chagrin, has been known to get a full year out of a ball of yarn.

## DUDLEY—WALKING ON WATER

≈

*By Gayle Portnow Halperin*
*Camden, Maine, and New York City, New York*

Our dog Dudley is Camden's enthusiastic (hyperactive) self-appointed canine greeter-of-neighbors-and-tourists. At two-and-a-half years, he's adorable, happy, funny, and totally endearing. He will always be a baby, or, more accurately, a toddler—adoring and adored, silly, misbehaving, fighting for control (of his leash), complying only when he wants to, needing constant attention, easily distracted, and hard to toilet train, or in his case, street train. We live in New York City most of the year, where all this behavior is exaggerated when he's walked.

Wheaten Terriers are known for their exuberance, and Dudley is true to nature, though perhaps extreme in his desire to kiss anyone who smiles at him; if you make eye contact, you'll get kissed. Most people respond with equal delight. He is very calm and gentle with children, allowing hugs and licking them sweetly while they pet him. He charms everyone but dog-haters.

He's such a happy, friendly creature, he's shocked if other dogs—especially large, loud ones off-leash or leaning out of open car windows—bark at him. Like a toddler, he hides behind me or my husband for protection, looking up with a perplexed expression, just not understanding why anyone would be mean to him. He is skittish, fearful of sudden loud noises—though not scared of thunder

*Dudley—source of wonder*
*and delight*

or fireworks—perhaps because a motorcycle on Atlantic Avenue in Camden frightened him when he was a puppy.

Before Dudley, we had Maxwell, a sweet, soulful, beautiful English Springer Spaniel. When he died at fifteen-and-a-half years, we knew we couldn't get another Springer, and since we'd almost gotten a Wheaten the first time, we chose Dudley. He couldn't be more different in personality and behavior if he were an elephant, but we love him with all our hearts.

I guess he sensed our feelings and thought he could walk on water. Last summer before coming to Maine, we visited friends in Westhampton Beach, Long Island. Their enclosed yard is one of the few places we can let Dudley run free, since he's rather autonomous about coming when called. While we sat on the deck chatting, he took off for their pool and was shocked and bewildered to find himself unable to skip across the surface. Frantic, trying to walk or swim, splashing wildly, he sank slowly into icy, chlorinated water, tangled in the folds of the heat-absorbing cover.

To his unpracticed eye, it must have looked traversable. Poor Dudley. We never found out if he could swim. Our host helped my husband pull him to safety, where he shook himself off onto his rescuers. Happily, he did not need mouth-to-mouth resuscitation, for that would have been a test of devotion few, if any, could pass.

Two weeks later I took him to Steamboat Landing in Camden, wanting to walk down to where the tide slaps noisily against the pebbled shore. He froze at the top of the ramp, terrified by the sight and/or sound of the water. He lurched back, pulling me away, and I could calm him only by leaving. For most of the time that summer I stood at the top of the hill, soothing him, petting him, luring him closer step-by-step, until he'd walked to the water's edge. Now it's hard to keep him away. I don't know if he's just being willful, or if he wants to try dog-paddling or nibbling seaweed and dead things, none of which would surprise me. Since his delicate stomach rules out snacking

on decay, and he won't let us
brush or bathe him and is afraid
of the hair-drier, immersion in
the bay is not an option. So I
struggle to drag him up the
ramp as he braces his legs and
tries to win our eternal tug
of war.

This summer Dudley is
afraid of the telephone and runs
to another room when it rings.
His idiosyncratic behavior makes
him a dear, funny, loving, well-
loved pet—a source of wonder
and delight.

*Surprised and wet but still ready
to give kisses*

Gayle Portnow Halperin lives in Camden, Maine, during summers and
winters in New York City. A sportswear designer-turned-photographer,
she took black-and-white photos of people for fifteen years, "concerned with revelation and obsessed with nuance and detail." Now she
looks for dogs who delight her, who show their emotions, who draw
her to them. Her first dog, an intuitive, expressive Springer Spaniel
named Maxwell, prompted her to keep her camera close and ready.
Like people, dogs can think and feel, she says, and her candid portraits
display a range of anthropomorphic expressions. Walking in
Westhampton Beach, her home on off-season weekends, she discovered several of her dog stars. But she photographs mostly on the streets
of New York City, fearless—she's been barked at only once—and
hopeful as she greets the chosen few with her camera. They always
surprise her.

# SMACK WATER JACK!

### By Nancy Benner-Gifford
#### Owls Head, Maine

Jack, our black Labrador Retriever, loves the water. It is in his nature. He is lucky, as we happen to live right in front of the ocean. During the summer months we can hardly keep him in the yard. He heads for the water first chance he gets. His favorite pastime is terrorizing the ducks that live in the cove. He thinks he will eventually catch one and boy, oh boy, then he will be the hunter he was born to be!

*Handsome "Jack Dog" of the Benner-Gifford family*

He has never bothered the blue herons that visit the shoreline. We wonder if he even sees them, as they tend to stand so tall and still in the water. Although we are sure he must smell them, he completely ignores them.

On the other hand, he plays in and with the seaweed, rolling in it, wrapping it around himself like a blanket. To him there is nothing like the smell of a pile of stinky seaweed rubbed all over his back. We call it his "seaweed massage." And if he gets lucky enough to find a crab in the seaweed, forget it—chomp, chomp. That will be one unlucky crab. He loves them, even though later he might regret it with a stomachache!

If you throw rocks into the water, he will love you forever. He darts and dives after them, not always returning with the same rock. But he doesn't care. A rock is a rock. As you can tell, "Jack Dog," as we sometimes call him, is a beloved member of our family. He has a great personality. If he ever lived a past life as a human, we imagine he might have lived the life of a pirate. Aye matey!

≋

Nancy Benner-Gifford lives in Owls Head, on the ocean. She was "born an artist," and that is still her work. She grew up in Rockland and moved to Portland in the late '70s, where she attended Portland School of Art. She stayed in Portland for almost twenty years, working in all phases of graphic arts, from print shops to ad agencies. She returned to Owls Head and is currently back in college full time to become an art teacher. At the time this story was written, Nancy Benner was a single mom with a twelve-year-old daughter. As we go to press, her daughter Rachel is fifteen years old, and Nancy is remarried—her husband Bill, a Rockland schoolteacher. "Of course, Jack Dog lives with us too," she says, "and, also, a rescued Shepherd named Katy."

# CHICA'S ODYSSEY

## By Alison Metcalfe
### Appleton, Maine

When my husband John and I were in our early, married years, we undertook what turned out to be a lengthy adventure that involved fixing up an old wooden boat and sailing it across the Atlantic. We took a circuitous route with prolonged stops in countries along the way. By the time we reached the northwest of Spain, two years after the boat was purchased, we had decided we wanted a pet.

An American friend brought us a small female tabby kitten with green eyes and round ears close to its head. Our friend told us that the owner of the mother cat and kittens had, for some unknown reason, clipped the points off the kitten's ears. This act of cruelty gave the kitten a highly distinctive appearance—she looked like a baby wildcat—and contributed, we felt, to her feisty personality. We called her "Chica."

*Chica looked like a baby wildcat*

Chica was as full of fun and pranks as any kitten. Left alone one day when we were on shore, she got hold of the end of a roll of toilet tissue and had the inside of the boat pretty well "tp'd" by the time we returned. She loved dinghy rides to the beach ("Wow! A giant sand-box!") and even rode in the rucksack on a backpacking trip.

*Totally at home with scratching posts as needed*

Worried that she would fall overboard, we decided that education was the better part of valor. We hung an old rope fender over the side, its lower end trailing in the water, and took the kitten for a dinghy ride. Rowing some distance away, we put Chica in the water. We felt our experiment was a success when she swam in a frantic dog-paddle straight for the boat, head held high, and scrambled up the fender, giving us a brief glimpse of what a skinny and undignified creature is a totally wet cat. From then on we were always careful to hang the rope fender overboard while in port. This enlargement of Chica's repertoire of accomplishments would later come back to haunt us.

Her first trip to sea proved Chica to be a die-hard old salt. She loathed the engine and expressed her disapproval of its racket with nerve-jangling shrieks. Heavy weather saw the boat's cat seated upright on the foredeck windlass, tail curled neatly around paws, swaying to the vessel's motion. The boat's people, oil-skinned and clipped to life-lines with safety harnesses, wrestled grimly with the slatting jib, flinching as the waves broke over them. Shouts of "Get below, Chica!" were disdainfully ignored. Chica learned to ignore the dollops of cold wet seawater that landed on her as she used her cockpit litter box. Such annoyances were clearly our fault. She took revenge by learning the difference between the sound of a flying fish flapping on deck and the slight knocks made by the block on the running stay, something we were unable to do. No wasted trips on deck in the middle of the night for Chica—and nothing but a fin or a tail to show in the morning.

By the time we reached the Canary Islands, Chica was old enough to come into season, and now it became apparent that our rope fender was like giving a teenager the keys to the car. Departure from Tenerife was delayed while we searched the waterfront and questioned local fishermen. After three days Chica appeared on the dock with loud demands to be picked up in the dinghy. She was very thin, desperately hungry, riddled with fleas, and pregnant. From then on we had to lock her in the head, the only cat-proof space on board, every time we prepared to leave a port.

The kittens, three of them, were born while we were in the Cape Verde Islands. The babies were healthy. Chica was a careful mother. All seemed set for a fair crossing until the moment of departure when everything came unglued in a way that can only happen on sailboats.

The anchor proved to be fouled, and we attempted to sail it out, with many approaches in a fresh breeze under full mainsail and jib, frantic sail and windlass work on my husband's part, much shouting and spinning of the wheel from me, and increasingly vocal complaints from Chica. Finally we gave up and started-ed the engine, getting the anchor out with a rush and freeing my husband to leap about lighting the kerosene running lights, for by now it was dusk.

Chica panicked at the engine's ruckus and started carrying

*Die-hard old salt*

her kittens one by one from below decks to the cockpit, where the tiny helpless things were at great risk of being rolled into the scuppers, caught up in a flapping rope, or being stepped on. While trying not to jibe and at the same time keep out of the way of an approaching ferry-boat, I picked up the kittens and put them inside my zippered jacket. Then I learned the truth that every mother knows— you need at least three hands to be a parent: one for the main sheet, one for the wheel, and one to hold the kittens in my jacket. Naturally appalled by their disappearance, Chica accused me in wailing tones. It was a great relief to get away from the harbor to the quietness of a night at sea in the trade winds.

Four cats and two people on a 40-foot boat for a trans-Atlantic crossing was altogether too many, but we made it safely to Trinidad. There we were able to find good homes for the kittens. Then on to Puerto Rico in expectation of the imminent arrival of our own little human "kitten." We moored in the small-boat channel in San Juan, with smooth concrete walls rising 10 feet from the water on either side—downstream the commercial harbor, and upstream, a long pull in the dinghy against a strong current, the marina.

Our pleasure in arriving there and meeting new friends was abruptly cut short when we returned to the boat one day to find no sign of Chica. Feeling wretchedly guilty, we remembered that we had not hung the rope fender overboard, because we had touched up the paint on the boat's topsides, and it was still not completely dry. Once again we scoured the waterfront, talked to the people at the marina, explained our plight to the kindly families at the Coast Guard base—a long way away, but the only possible landing place. We even put an ad in the paper. Sadly, we had to conclude that Chica had drowned. In pursuit of carnal delights, she must have tried to swim ashore. But no little cat could climb those retaining walls or swim the long distance against the current to reach the Coast Guard base or make it to the marina.

Fast-forward nine months. During this period Merchant Mariner John works for five months on a Farrell Lines ship going to Africa. We have a baby son, with whom I travel for three months, showing the baby off to grandparents on both sides of "The Pond." We move the boat to the other end of Puerto Rico Island, at Isleta Marina near Fajardo. We own and lose to illness another cat. While living aboard the boat at Isleta, we decide to take the publico (taxi-bus) to San Juan for the day to take care of various business matters. Our errands taken care of, we stroll down the dock of the marina to visit friends. Ahead of us, also strolling down the dock, is a desperately scrawny tabby cat that looks rather like a small wildcat. I say to my husband, "That cat looks just like Chica," and we

*Chica snuggling in*

start to call her by name. The cat turns and runs straight to us, purring until she almost chokes, twining around our legs, begging to be picked up, which we do, tearfully and unbelievingly.

We nursed Chica back to health with the assistance of a sympathetic and nautically-minded veterinarian who made boat calls and also gave us a group rate on having Chica and two cats on a neighboring Norwegian boat spayed. She lived with us for four more years and made the homeward-bound leg of our long voyage to my husband's hometown of Marblehead, Massachusetts. Swallowing the anchor to move ashore was no problem for Chica. She loved the new opportunities opened up by yard and woods. We rented homes in a quiet suburb and on a blueberry hillside.

Chica saw us through the arrival of two more children and became a dutiful, if grumpy, nursemaid. We got dirty looks if the baby cried, and Chica would supervise the little boys in their outdoor play.

From boat, to two years on Cape Cod, to two years in a rented house in Maine, Chica was a vivid personality in our daily lives. But two weeks after we moved into our own home, she was killed by a car traveling the busy road on which the house was situated. She had no traffic experience to guide her. Unlike being on the water, we could teach Chica no techniques to cope with the road, and she would not tolerate being confined to the house. We buried her in the backyard with tears from all the family, knowing that her death truly marked the end of a remarkable chapter in our lives.

Alison Metcalfe is a native of Scotland and graduated with an M.A. (Honors) from Edinburgh University. With her American husband, John, she lived on a boat for five years, spending time in the south of England, Spain, Portugal, Madeira, and the Canary and Cape Verde Islands before crossing the Atlantic under sail in 1972. After moving ashore, she lived two years on Cape Cod before coming to Maine, where the family settled in Union. Since 1986 Alison has worked as the office manager at Rockland Congregational Church. She is active in the Union Historical Society, the Vose Library, and People's United Methodist Church in Union. Her interests are reading, history, spending time with family, canoeing, and travel. The Metcalfes now live in Appleton, Maine, and have three grown children and two grandchildren. They still keep (or are kept by) pet cats.

## FUNDY—A WORK IN PROGRESS

※

### By Lolly and Jim Mitchell
#### Camden, Maine

Cruising with Fundy is still a "work in progress." He was born in October 1999, and, at the time of this writing, we have had only one summer season together. Perhaps the real story is our search for the ideal cruising pet!

*Fundy—ready for adventure—Let's go!*

For the past twenty-five years we had bred Golden Retrievers. The last of the line, our beloved Sassy, never liked the water much. In fact we had to teach her to swim in a pool. Although she tolerated being on board our boat, she inevitably got seasick and suffered stoically for the entire passage. So when she died in June 1999 at age fourteen, we decided to look for a smaller dog. Soaking-wet 80-pounders are very difficult to get aboard.

However, the future pet had to be a REAL dog—not a cat that barks!

Our search began in the dog book section at the Camden Public Library. Lo and behold we found a breed from Nova Scotia that resembles a Golden but is half the size. A phone call to a friend at the Lunenburg Foundry provided personal confirmation, as her sister has one. An Internet search led us to three breeders, and, through e-mail messages to the breeders, we located a litter in Stubenacadie, a rural community between Halifax and Truro at the head of the Bay of

Fundy. So, last November we drove 1,000 miles in two days to meet our three-week-old puppy.

Once called "Little River Duck Dogs," this breed was developed in Nova Scotia. The dogs specialize in waterfowl, because their onshore antics lure curious birds within firing range. Then the dogs retrieve the downed

*Safe and happy aboard* Kintore

birds. "Tolling" is the name for this technique, which resembles a trick used by the fox. That is why the breed was originally thought to be a fox/retriever mix, although this is genetically impossible. The breed is a mixture of Retriever, Spaniel, Setter and Collie, perfected in the latter half of the 19th century. Recognized by the Canadian Kennel Club in 1945, the breed was christened "Nova Scotia Duck Tolling Retriever."

According to Allene White, who breeds Golden Retrievers in Brooklin, Maine, and whose late husband, Joel, built our previous boat, we can expect Fundy to proudly present us with buoys, mooring balls, and the occasional lobster trap. In the meantime he has become a strong swimmer, loves to ride in the bow of the launch, and has almost mastered the art of jumping on and off the boat. But best of all, he loves to go!

≋

Fundy's parents are Lolly and Jim Mitchell who arrived in Camden by boat in 1989. In a previous life they founded Sakonnet Vineyards in Little Compton, Rhode Island, and operated it for thirteen years. In addition to tending 45 acres of vines and producing 20,000 gallons of delicious wine on an annual basis, they raised over 100 Golden Retriever pups – "as a cash crop," they say.

Prior to those "vintage years" Jim enjoyed several careers in industry—initially as an engineer with Union Carbide Company, then as USAID Advisor to the Korean Government, and finally as an International Consultant with Arthur D. Little, where he worked primarily on energy projects in the Middle East. A terrorist attack on his aircraft in Rome in 1973 convinced the Mitchells to find a safer lifestyle!

Meanwhile Lolly spent eighteen years working as a publicist for architects, including Walter Gropius, at The Architects Collaborative in Cambridge, Massachusetts, as well as John Carl Warnecke in San Francisco, California, and Washington, D.C., where she handled the press relations for the John F. Kennedy Grave in Arlington, Virginia.

Today, Lolly and Jim say they are "very happy living in an old Maine farmhouse overlooking beautiful Penobscot Bay, taking care of one boat, one garden, one dog and one cat."

## SUSIE, FLYKA, AND MUFFINS—HAPPY MEMORIES

*By Esther Maria Hardy*
*Hope, Maine*

My family loved to travel and especially enjoyed camping. Susie, my sweet gray-and-white cat, and Flyka, my beloved dog, were always with us, enjoying it as much as we did.

Both are in pet heaven now, where they have joined all of our former pets.

Susie, at the age of fourteen, left us after suffering from arthritis and partial paralysis of her hindquarters. She went peacefully in my arms, our compassionate veterinarian standing by. I

*Susie, enjoying one of her favorite pastimes*

like to think she was dreaming of how she loved to get on a float in our swimming pool, enjoying herself as we pushed her about.

Maybe she learned this from our beautiful Border Collie, Flyka, who also loved to ride on a float. Sometimes we would tip her off, and she would swim to the stairs, climb out, then sit on the deck drying out while waiting for us to join her.

Flyka also loved to run along the beach, but only where the waves broke so she could try to catch them.

Susie and Flyka were important parts of our lives. Susie was a sweet kitten when she was given to me by my daughter Lily. Flyka, whose name means "girl" in Swedish, was given to me by a friend while we were working together as nurses. During the years we had them, my husband and I traveled as much as possible, and they were always with us in our motor homes and trailers. At the age of sixteen, Flyka joined Susie in heaven—together, perhaps, in some great campground in the sky.

As I look back over the years, I remember, also, our pet dog Muffins, who loved to ride around in our row-boat for hours. She was always eager to do this.

*Flyka — just resting or awaiting her turn?*

When we began to prepare for a boat ride, she would run to the lake and jump into the boat before we did. Always joyful and enthusiastic about such outings, she, too, was a wonderful companion.

We treasure all of these happy memories of our water-loving pets and want to share them with you.

Esther Maria Hardy, born to Swedish immigrant parents in 1914, grew up in the Boston area and moved to Walpole, Massachusetts, after her marriage to Edward Hardy. During World War II, Esther was a Red Cross volunteer. She then went to nursing school, became an L.P.N., and worked in various hospitals. In 1975, the Hardys retired to Maine. Edward died in 1997, but Esther remains in their Maine home, where she lives with youngest daughter Lily, and Lily's cat Ginger. Besides one other daughter and two sons, Esther has seventeen grandchildren, thirty-six great grandchildren, and two great, great grandchildren. She enjoys flower gardening, painting, sketching, sewing, cooking, reading, knitting, and needlework.

# RUDI AND THE LOBSTER BUOY

≈

## By Richard Crowell, M.S., D.V.M.
### Medfield Veterinary Clinic, Medfield, Massachusetts

Rudi is my seven-year-old black Labrador Retriever—retriever with a capital R. Since she was a puppy she's loved to do two things: eat and retrieve. I cannot recall training her to bring things back to me, but it seems she has always done that. She retrieves quickly but is slow to hand off the retrieved item unless food is an option.

Rudi's favorite place to retrieve is in the ocean. My parents have a beautiful summer home in the small town of North Falmouth, Massachusetts, on Buzzards Bay. Too rocky for swimmers, a quiet beach in front of their home is visited occasionally by a few striper fishermen at sunset.

Since lobsters like the numerous small crevices and nooks in which to hide, hunt, and live, this rocky beach is an excellent location to place lobster traps. To make the lobster traps sink, bricks are placed in the steel wire enclosures. Then long lengths of rope with Styrofoam buoys are attached to the traps. These buoys present a problem for Rudi.

Three years ago on a clear, mild, spring day with air temperatures around 60 degrees, I went for a hike along this rocky coast. In just a few minutes Rudi had jumped into the ocean to cool off. Floating like a senior citizen in the movie *Cocoon*, she could not have been happier.

Rudi was already wet; so I decided to have her retrieve a decoy buoy, the kind duck hunters use to train dogs to retrieve waterfowl. Unfortunately, the decoy buoys look a lot like lobster buoys. When Labs get out in the open water with waves and large amounts of reflected sunlight, they sometimes become confused. This was the case for Rudi, who went for a lobster buoy instead of the decoy buoy. I

*Rudi in her favorite place with her favorite toy—*

watched Rudi do this, thinking she would figure out her mistake and find the real retrieval buoy shortly. Alas, she latched onto the lobster buoy and started tugging. It was a little bigger than the other buoy but fit into her mouth quite well.

Seconds turned into minutes. First I tried to call her in. That didn't work. Next I tried to divert her attention by throwing other things for her to retrieve. Again, no luck. I even tried to tempt her with food, but she was stubborn. After ten minutes of Rudi's version of water aerobics, I knew I had to do something before she tired herself out.

I quickly ran up to the house, changed into a bathing suit and swam into the frigid water. I was numb instantly. And she was still trying

*—a decoy buoy*

her best to retrieve that buoy. When I reached her and gently pulled the buoy out of her mouth, she seemed relieved that her job was completed. I guided her to shore, where she did a quick shake and, never discouraged, started scouring the beach for more things to retrieve.

Rudi is a great companion, and I enjoy swimming with her every summer. But I try to avoid swims in the cooler seasons. And I never throw a duck buoy before June 15th.

~~~

Dr. Richard Crowell received his bachelor's degree in biology from
Fairfield University, a master's degree in biology from Boston College,
and his doctorate in veterinary medicine from Tufts University School
of Veterinary Medicine. Dr. Crowell is a member of the American
Veterinary Medical Association (AVMA), the American Animal
Hospital Association (AAHA), and the Massachusetts Veterinary
Medical Association (MVMA). He is married and has four children.
At the time this story was written he also had two dogs (Rudi and
Gillie) and two rabbits (Cottontail and Nippers).

*The following story is a slightly abridged version of an article first published in* Points East, *May 1999, under the title,* It's a Dog's Life. *It is reproduced here, courtesy of* Points East, The Gulf of Maine Cruising Magazine, *with permission of the author.*

## BLACK HAIRS IN THE COCKPIT
## PART I

≋

### By Nina M. Scott
*Amherst, Massachusetts, and Friendship, Maine*

My older brother Norman, a fine, experienced sailor and a man of almost unlimited virtues, loves to come to Maine and sail with us out of Friendship. But a few summers ago, he surveyed our white topside and remarked in a voice of distinct disapproval, "My God, how do you stand all these black hairs in the cockpit?"

OK, so there are clumps of them here and there, but Jim and I are so used to them that they really don't bother us. Black Labradors are just a part of our family, and the different ones we've had—along with the boats that accompanied them—mark milestones in our lives.

Schatzi was our first, my wedding present to Jim. She was Oregon-bred (we were living in California at the time) and at first was very afraid of water, having had a bad experience as a pup, we gathered. By the time we got her to Maine she was fine. She enjoyed sailing and turned out to be a fine swimmer, with that characteristic high Lab leap into the water. At that point, Jim owned a clunky wooden center-boarder of undistinguished lines, about 18 feet long, built by Carleton Simmons, the Friendship postmaster. She was heavy, slow, and her rudder was too small, but Jim and his friends had had a lot of fine hours in her when he was growing up in Friendship.

Bridget, Schatzi's successor, got to sail in the *One Club*, the O'Day

Daysailer we had from 1966 until 1993 (named that in honor of Jim's father's favorite opening bid at bridge. He was a crack bridge player, but his son was always a better sailor.) Bridget was a sweet girl, but a wimp about swimming and boating. She would wade into the water up to her elbows, rarely farther. Very embarrassing. She had a gig where she would let other dogs swim out after sticks, meet them a few feet from shore, take the stick from them, and bring it to us, proud as Punch.

Worse, she was a pain when out on the boat and bored. Generally, she would begin to whine when we were about two-and-a-half hours out, and the rest of the sail was not a lot of fun.

The dog pendulum swung in the opposite direction with Charlotte, a consummate sailor if ever there was one. Good swimmer, too, and so competitive that if she and another dog were after a ball or a stick in the water and the other dog got it first, she would put on a burst of speed, climb aboard the other dog's back until his head went under water and he'd have to let go of the stick. She would then retrieve it and head for shore, very proud of herself.

Charlotte spanned time on the O'Day and on *Caledonian*, the Pearson Triton we own now. Jim and I managed to capsize the *One Club* about four times in the long time we sailed her. This was always a major hassle, as she turned turtle each time and was impossible to right without help. The last time we went over, Charlotte was get-

*Charlotte—consummate sailor and retriever of other dogs' treasures—home harbor, Muscle Ridge Channel*

ting a tad arthritic when getting in and out of boats. I was on the starboard rail when the puff came and over we went. I had to dive to stay free of the boat. I surfaced with my prescription sunglasses still miraculously on my nose, but I was definitely encumbered by sweater and slicker.

Jim had somehow walked over the hull as it went over and was sitting by the centerboard, wet only from the waist down. The water wasn't too cold, and I held onto the hull, treading water. My first thought was for Charlotte. "Jim! Jim! Where's Charlotte?" I yelled, fearing she might have been pinned under the boat. Even though we were in sight of our cottage and someone would come get us, I was worried about her having to swim so long with her old legs. "She's over on the other side," Jim said, and even while he was speaking I saw her round the stern and come towards me, towing a rope in her mouth to bring to me. In the midst of all that confusion, she had thought first of us. I hugged her neck, and we hauled her aboard the overturned hull, where she sat in total calm and composure, braced against the centerboard, until help came.

Charlotte got used to the 28-foot *Caledonian* and her much larger dimensions with no difficulty. When she got hot in the sunshine on deck she would hop down the companionway and jump up on one of the bunks, where she would bag out contentedly for hours. She was also quick to pick up on the fact that when the wind increased and the boat began to heel she could hop from bunk to bunk to be on the lee side, so that she wouldn't slide off. When the decks would really tilt, she wedged herself into the space on the floor between the bunks, where she was braced on all sides. Somehow, she just knew these things.

Charlotte was so in love with sailing that she simply would not tolerate our even thinking of leaving her ashore. We made our first short forays into cruising Muscongus Bay with her: Harbor Island, High Harbor in Muscle Ridge Channel, Tenants Harbor, and Port Clyde. In spite of aging joints, she never lost heart or her love of the sea. She was a trooper until the day she died in 1996.

Having been thoroughly spoiled by Charlotte, we expected Hannah, our present Lab, to be a natural as well, especially because she was Maine-born. Hannah is drop-dead gorgeous, with a feisty personality and much charm. She came to Friendship when she was less than a year old, and Jim and I discovered right away that Hannah was NOT a natural boat dog. She really made us realize how frightening coming aboard a boat can be for a young dog—tilting, slippery seats off which one slides with a great scraping of toenails; sails that slat and pop when coming about; and lots of lines to stay clear of and not chew. Then there's the drill of getting in and out of the *Dog Bone* (our dinghy) and suppressing the desire to retrieve mackerel off the hook when we fished. Hannah was anxious and frightened the first few times out and did what all anxious dogs do: shed copious amounts of hair.

We spent the entire summer of 1997 slowly and patiently getting Hannah comfortable with *Caledonian*. It cut into our cruising schedule, but having a happy dog aboard was more important to us. And learn she did, though she still hasn't picked up on Charlotte's trick of bunk hopping when the boat is heeling. Hannah now thoroughly enjoys herself by running forward and being alpha dog on the bow, has stopped chewing on the jib-sheets, and has trained us to sail with the dodger up because she likes it on deck but out of the sun.

*Hannah (right) following in Charlotte's competitive footsteps—with best friend Simone*

But what she really likes is island hopping, and since she needs to relieve herself every five hours or so, we just work that into our sail plan. Because of her, we have gone ashore and explored islands we would otherwise just have sailed by without stopping. We discovered magic places in our bay: Black and Otter Islands, with soft moss underfoot, the sweet scent of balsam, the crash of waves against the rocks, the cries of gull, tern, and osprey. Birch Island in Muscle Ridge Channel is a favorite, as is the lovely curved beach at Little Burnt. The trails across Harbor Island are decorated by little fairy altars, or gnome homes—small structures made of sticks, shells, or stones, and decorated with Spanish moss and mussel shells. No one disturbs these shrines to the spirit of the beautiful islands.

Because of Hannah's exuberant nature, Jim and I have had many fascinating conversations with the folks we meet on these island walks—hardy young Outward Bounders, experienced old salts, families with children, lone kayakers, and, of course, other dog owners. Sailing into Little Burnt last summer, there were four boats anchored there that had dogs aboard, all Labs. We all agreed that having a dog aboard was more work, but also more fun.

Last summer, Hannah was so anxious to get on deck one morning that she failed to remember the screen over the hatch. Giving a great bound up the companion stairs, she bonked against the screen and fell back onto my bunk with a crash—a Keystone Cops routine that had Jim and me laughing until we had tears in our eyes. Hannah was not amused.

Aside from the comic relief, sailing with Hannah has another advantage: she is very useful aboard when it comes to meal cleanup. Jim calls it the "canine pre-rinse cycle."

So now, by dint of love and patience, we once again have another good boat dog. And we have more black hairs in the cockpit. But we can live with that. Anchoring for the night in some lovely bay, breaking out the wine and cheese, and having Hannah curl up next to you and put her head lovingly on your knee—well, it just doesn't get much better than that.

*The following slightly altered contribution was first published in* Points East,
*May 1999, without authorship shown. It is reproduced here, courtesy of*
Points East, *The Gulf of Maine Cruising Magazine,*
*with permission of the author.*

## MAKING THE TRANSITION: BISCUITS HELP PART II

≈

### By Jim Scott
*Amherst, Massachusetts, and Friendship, Maine*

Now to the problem at hand: How do you get a big dog into and out of a small dinghy for those necessary trips to shore? And is it really worth it?

The answer to the second question is easy. Yes! I am the one who usurps this wonderful occasion to venture ashore with Hannah, as I did with her three predecessors. At dawn or at dusk to row to a Maine island, to walk the shingle beach or climb the spine of Birch Island in Muscle Ridge Channel and watch the sunrise or sunset through the clouds with the sound of the seabirds mingled with the sweep of the sea on the rocks below, and look out at the lobster boats at work in the bay is always rewarding, if unpredictable.

It is an opportunity for enrichment of the soul. There was the time we, Hannah and I, discovered a half-decayed seal wedged between the low-tide rocks of Hall Island. Yuck! This required strong master-dog discipline. Then there was the discovery of the gnome homes on Harbor Island, constructed by unknown wanderers on this island before us. Or the delicacy of the spider's web across the path at dawn, laced with pearls of dew in the morning sunlight. These are the wonders that await the sailor who has a dog aboard.

Such are the rewards for those awkward moments when a 70-pound Labrador leaps from the deck of the boat into your arms in the

8-foot dinghy and you struggle to avoid a group swim in the icy water.

So how do you get that 70-pound Lab into and out of that 8-foot dinghy from the deck of a 28-foot sailing cruiser?

The ultimate result has been that Hannah simply hops from the deck of the *Caledonian* onto the center seat of the dinghy and curls up in the stern floor space for the rowing trip to or from shore. Upon return, with the painter secured around the starboard sheet winch, she vaults from the middle seat over the rail and into the cockpit.

To reach this state of bliss required many "learning experiences" for both man and beast. Initially, it was the "grunt" stage, in which the smaller puppy was bodily lifted from one craft to the other in order that the human participants could get onto the water and go sailing. The next step was the "re-entry" phase, because it is easier to jump down from the boat into the dinghy than up from the dinghy into the boat.

Slowly, by placing paws on the edge of the deck with assistance in the stern quarters, the dog more or less quickly learned that it was possible, and worth it, by a liberal sprinkling of dog biscuits on the cockpit seats, to scale in a single bound this wall of blue fiberglass into the unseen cockpit. You have to realize that Labradors have

*Hannah, aboard* Caledonian, *High Harbor, Muscle Ridge Channel*

a ninety-five percent orientation toward their stomachs. We devoted the whole summer of 1997 to "educating" Hannah in the fine art of sailing and cruising. As with any off-spring, you invest huge quantities of time, effort, and mostly love into this individual with whom you selfishly want to share some of life's most satisfying moments. For us, those are the ones while we are sailing.

*Hannah with Jim aboard* Caledonian, *Harbor Island, Muscongus Bay—It just doesn't get much better than this*

Nina Scott is a professor of Spanish American literature at the University of Massachusetts at Amherst. Her husband, Jim, is a retired high school and college chemistry teacher. Summers are spent in Friendship, Maine. The Scotts are avid sailors and Lab owners—beginning with Schatzi, Nina's wedding gift to Jim. They say they "have loved each of them dearly and, for more than forty years, have taken one and all sailing."

# ZACK—A TRUE DOGGY FISH STORY

## By Jean Weinstein
### River Road, Cushing, Maine

My husband and I got Zack when he was about two years old. A relative of mine is a veterinarian, and Zack, a former patient, had been brought in as an abandoned stray. The owners could not be located; so when I went in looking for a dog to adopt, there was our boy—ready and waiting.

He was a joy, licking my face on the way home from the clinic. He had been named Zig Zag because of his running style, but we re-named him "Zachary," which seemed more gentlemanly to us.

When my husband and I moved to Maine from New Hampshire ten years ago, Zachary discovered and loved salt water, something he hadn't had in New Hampshire. At first he loved just standing in it, although, eventually, he did learn to swim.

"Zack," as we called him, was a Shepherd/Terrier mix with big Shepherd ears, and the coarse hair, chin whiskers, short legs and tail of a Scottish Terrier. He became our constant companion. His only bad habit was excessive barking at everyone who came to the house. It was appreciated when I was alone, however. My husband had to return to New Hampshire quite often on business.

Zack was a great watchdog. He never strayed or needed a leash. He was very active, loved walks, chasing squirrels, and playing with other dogs his size. Trudy, a Basset Hound who liked our neighborhood better than her own, and Angus, our neighbor's Sheltie, were his favorites.

*Never another one like our Zack*

*Zack and his "dad" waiting for the big bite*

One day not too long after we had moved to Maine, my husband was enjoying one of his rare fishing days off the end of our floating dock on the Georges River. He had just caught a nice-sized mackerel and dropped it into the bucket beside him, where it flipped and flopped wildly. Zack, with ears pricked, watched the performance with much interest.

Suddenly, with one great flip, over the side of the bucket and into the river went the fish. Zack jumped up, ran up the ramp and down the steps and into the water. Now all Zack had ever done before was wade in carefully, and stand or swim a short distance after a thrown stick. This time he had to get the escaped fish for his "dad."

Out past the dock he swam, around the other side, looking left and right, determined to find the escapee. Finally, I worried that the whole effort would be too much for our fat dog, who was six years old at the time, and I called him back. He came, but he was still looking around when he waded ashore. Could there be a bit of retriever in his mixed-breed background? Perhaps not. He didn't have such an incentive again. We did appreciate his heroic efforts at the time, though.

As he grew older, aches and pains slowed him down. He would be content just to wade in and stand in the cold salt water. It must have felt good on his arthritic old legs.

We lost him in January of 2001, after a stroke, a six-day hospital stay, and two weeks of home nursing. He was fourteen years old. We were heartbroken. Never another one like our Zack.

≋

Jean Weinstein was brought up on the shores of Lake Sunapee, New Hampshire, where her grandfather was a fishing guide. She and her husband have always loved the water. They had a Chris-Craft cruiser on the lake that always had their dogs aboard when they took it out. After vacationing in Maine for twenty years and loving it, they moved to the state in 1991. They still love Maine and the saltwater. Jean enjoys gardening, knitting, reading, and a new interest—kayaking. She and her husband are semi-retired and thoroughly enjoying their current location. They bought another old Chris-Craft boat that they are restoring.

## BAMBI—THE FISHERMAN'S DOG

### By Deborah J. Norwood
#### Rockland, Maine

Bambi was a black Cocker Spaniel that wet on my dad's lap the first time they met. "No," my dad said. "We sure don't need another dog." But Bambi, named after the Disney deer, stayed. He came right into the family to share in many boating adventures.

We had a big family; so our family outings usually involved going to an island for picnics during the summer months or taking other special trips. Sometimes we would go to the Boothbay-Bristol area to join my uncle and his family. Then we would all go together for a picnic somewhere. Wonderful!

One time my dad, mother, and I took Bambi with us on a boat trip to Boston Light, the place of my dad's youth. After we anchored, Bambi and I took the rowboat and rowed ashore to sight-see. Water dog that he was by nature, Bambi loved being with us on such trips. But, as pleasant as such excursions were, Bambi was a fisherman's dog.

My dad Bruce Norwood was a fisherman—lobsters, scallops, a few shrimp, crabs, sometimes even a sea sponge; something different to bring home after a day's work with Bambi at his heels.

This relationship developed after Bambi passed a test my dad gave him. The spaniel loved the ocean; so whenever my dad's behavior even suggested going to the shore, Bambi was waiting. My dad challenged him one morning, saying, "Get my slippers or boots if you want to go." Bambi did. He passed the test, and they became fishing partners after that.

The dog knew his place on the skiff. He also knew my dad's commands: "Wait" (until I pull in the skiff). "Jump" (from skiff to boat). "Stay—cold water" (in case the dog saw a gull he wanted to taste or chase).

Every once in a while my dad told a favorite Bambi story. It seems the traps were hauling an abundance of large crabs. They were scurrying about the floor. All these scurrying "things" with all those legs caught Bambi's eye. He knew enough to keep his distance. He could move his nose away quite quickly, but oh, those long ears!

When a crab clamped his crusher claw onto one of those ears, Bambi shook his head and shook and shook, to no avail. Dad went to the rescue, freeing the ear from the claw. He always used to chuckle when he recalled this incident with Bambi and the crab.

Both dad and Bambi have gone now. I like to think they're together on that boat again.

≋

Deborah Norwood was born in Rockland in the city's Knox Hospital, which now functions as the Knox Center for Long Term Care. She is an L.P.N. there. She lives by the ocean and enjoys a daily walk with her dog Chloé. As a young child, it was she who named the dog in the story "Bambi." Although Bambi was her dog, Deborah's dad and the spaniel shared wonderful companionship—"truly a remarkable bond as strong and deep as the sea, itself."

# OUT TO SEA

≋

## By Stanley E. Silva
### Union, Maine

I was born and raised in California and lived in the small coastal town of Pacific Grove on Monterey Bay. For twenty years, I had a small sign shop there, about five blocks from the apartment where my wife and I lived. I usually walked to and from work, enjoying the walk along the ocean at Pacific Grove beach.

On one of these walks, as I took in the sunshine, ocean, and smell of the sea, I heard a dog barking. This, in itself, meant nothing, but the sound was coming from the wrong direction, and as I continued to hear it, it became more of a puzzle. I stopped and paid more attention to the barking, which was barely audible over the sound of the waves crashing on the rocks across the road from me.

Curiosity made me cross the road, and as I stood by the guardrail on the other side, I saw a strange sight. Out in the kelp beds, about 100 feet offshore, was a black Labrador Retriever, swimming and barking. This dog was clearly having fun, but was a quarter of a mile from the beach and heading out to sea. Then, as I looked further ahead of the dog, 50 feet or so, I realized what was happening. Up ahead a sea otter was swimming along on its back. The sea otter would stop occasionally and look back at the dog as if in disbelief, then swim a little further. As I stood there watching, another sound came to me. The dog's owner was on the beach frantically calling his pet.

All in all this was a strange sight, and it made me smile. The Lab was very excited and not about to give up, but, clearly, there was no way he could ever catch a sea otter in its own environment. I knew the dog would soon tire and be in big trouble. I watched for a while and then walked along to the beach. Another person, who also had been watching, told me that the Coast Guard had been called and was on the way around the point from the main harbor in Monterey. There were no boats at Pacific Grove beach.

The next day I heard the happy ending. The Coast Guard had rescued the dog. But I will never forget that day and the humor inherent in the situation—a dog joyfully trying to out-swim a sea otter.

〰

Stanley Silva, known by many as "Stan," was born in Hayward, California, but was raised and educated in Pacific Grove, which is on the Monterey Peninsula. He loved to fish off the rocks along the Big Sur coastline and to hunt, fish, and camp in the Sierra Nevada Mountains. He is committed to caring for this world in order to pass it on to our children.

Stan feels that he was "born an artist"—a gift from God—which allowed him to run his California sign shop for more than twenty years before moving to Union, where his two children were born. He still loves art, has lived "a relatively quiet life" and presently works at Wayfarer Marine in Camden. He recently restarted his sign business in Union but has added a variety of other artistic products, including metal sculpture and decorative ironwork for the home.

## SOMETHING ABOUT PIRATE

≋

*By Maggie Johnston*
Mount Desert, Maine

Pirate was a most unusual cat who, from the beginning, craved adventure. He was aptly named—an orange and white tiger kitten with a patch of black hair over one eye. At the age of two he was blinded in that black-patched eye as a result of a car accident. His recovery was miraculous but, curiously, added an even more "pirate-like" dimension to his appearance.

Pirate came into our lives when we were wanting a boat cat. One of my students had a cat named "Herbie," who had kittens. When they became available, we felt the time had arrived. I went to Herbie's home at a lobster fisherman's house to look at the litter when the kittens were only four weeks old. At that time the kitten who would become Pirate followed me to the door as if to say "I want to come home with you." We wanted him from the beginning, but he seemed a little too adventurous to settle in as a laid-back boat cat; so we decided to take his brother instead. But the brother was given to another family, and Pirate was destined to have his way. Two weeks later as the remaining kittens were being loaded into a laundry basket for

*Pirate in command aboard* Chamar *off Cape Rosier*

their fateful trip to the SPCA, I received a phone call at school and was told to intercept them in front of the church on High Road in ten minutes.

Once again Pirate claimed possession of us, and I took him home to a household that was ill-prepared to meet his needs that night. He became part of our lives, and we shared in his many adventures—some of which caused us great worry.

The kitten, far too young to be left home alone, spent his first two days with us in a dry aquarium at Mount Desert Elementary School where my husband Bill taught. On the second day Pirate figured out how to climb over the side of the aquarium, offering a hint of escapades to come.

At the time Pirate adopted us we had a 22-foot Friendship Sloop, *Magi*, we had planned to sail to the annual Friendship Sloop Regatta in Friendship, Maine. We spent several weeks trying to get Pirate accustomed to sailing on a small boat before our first trip from Northeast Harbor to Friendship. From that point on, our adventures with Pirate, both going and coming home from these annual regattas, have been many and memorable, two of which I share with you.

## PIRATE'S FRIENDSHIP CAPER

When we sailed our small boat into Friendship Harbor and saw all the other sloops, we wondered how we would ever be able to become acquainted with other boat owners and their crews. We need not have worried. Pirate was our key. Who could resist an adorable kitten? Certainly not the children.

We had barely anchored when children from both *Resolute* and *Tannis* rowed by wanting to know the particulars of the arrival of this new little sloop. Pirate, always a friendly sort, promptly made himself known to the children, and a love affair was born.

In the afternoon after the races, the children got into their dories and rowed over to *Magi* to visit their new friend, Pirate, and his human friends, Bill and Maggie. Ted, Debbie, and Harold from *Resolute* and Carolyn, Billy, Wayne, and Jeff from *Tannis* brought Tad from *Phoenix* for regular visits. They even invited Pirate and his persons to a cookout on Friendship Long Island a couple of nights later.

The parents of all these children wanted to know the attraction of this tiny sloop. So, on the second afternoon of the kids' visits, their parents arrived to check out what was happening. With so many people aboard, water came in through the cockpit drains, and we had a fleeting fear that *Magi* might sink. But Pirate's friendly nature has helped us form many lasting friendships during the years we cruised the Maine coast, from Mount Desert Island to Friendship, aboard the *Magi*.

*The author, with Pirate as scout,*
*rowing toward a shore adventure*

## CALAMITY AT PORT CLYDE

The calamity at Port Clyde occurred on one of our annual trips to the Friendship Sloop Regatta, when we anchored for the night near a burned-out lobster dock. Pirate dearly loved seafood, particularly lobster and clams, and reveled in any scents associated with them. During the hours before sunset, he had been eagerly watching the shore and sniffing the enticing aromas from the lobster dock in anticipation of a gourmet treat.

Generally, when we turned in for the night, Pirate was free to sleep below or prowl the decks. On this occasion we were awakened shortly after midnight by a loud splash. Trying to get close to those wonderful smells, Pirate had leaned so far over the side of the hull that he fell overboard. We immediately launched a rescue search.

I jumped into the dinghy dressed only in T-shirt and skivvies, grateful for the darkness. Bill searched the waters with *Magi*'s flashlight as I desperately called Pirate's name. I had almost reached the shore when Pirate answered me, but his meow wasn't coming from the land. I rowed in circles as I searched. Finally, I found him on the top of a burned piling.

What a dilemma! The tide was low, so it was difficult to grasp the barnacle-encrusted piling, let alone climb it. Pirate was well ensconced on the very top and had no intention of coming down—even with a great amount of coaxing. I finally decided to row back to the *Magi* to get clothing and husband Bill's help. When the dinghy was about six feet from the piling, Pirate started to climb down. I rowed back and grabbed him when he came within range.

Pirate seemed unaffected by his encounter with the briny deep, but it took two weeks for my hands to heal from barnacle cuts caused by trying to hold onto the piling. The lesson learned from this story? Keep Pirate below during the hours of darkness.

Pirate sailed with us for sixteen years, on board *Magi* and then *Chamar.* He was a great cat and has forever touched our hearts. It was truly difficult to say goodbye to this fine friend. He died in March of 1993. We missed him so much that the next month, we adopted Port and Starboard from the Bangor Humane Society. We felt that two would be required to replace our beloved Pirate.

≈≈≈

When Maggie Johnston wrote this story, she was a second grade teacher at Pemetic School in Southwest Harbor, Maine. She retired in June of 2002, her first opportunity, she says, to indulge her creative interests in writing and painting. During the summer months she and her husband Bill, both U.S. Coast Guard-licensed captains, own and operate Great Harbor Charters, sailing from Northeast Harbor, Maine. They ply the waters off Mount Desert Island in the company of their feline crew: first, Port and Starboard, who assumed Pirate's responsibilities; then Port and Miss Matey, who offers comfort following the unexpected loss of Starboard to a heart condition on the day of Maggie's retirement in 2002. Maggie's hope, following her retirement from teaching young children, is to write a children's book about Pirate's adventures and those of Port, Starboard, Miss Matey, and others who may follow.

# JEB'S STORY

*By Mary B. Morrissey*
*North Brookfield, Massachusetts*

J eb was born and bred on Penobscot Bay. It's a whale of a tale, all
true, about the escapades of this remarkably intelligent, water-
loving dog, an enthusiast of water sports, both fresh and salt.
Jeb was formerly known as "Zeb," short for "Zebulon." One spring
day nine years ago he found himself at the Camden-Rockport Animal
Shelter just in time for his second birthday. Out-of-state visitors happened by after hearing good things about the shelter and its caring
staff. The handsome, yellow, retriever-mix was sitting by a tree,

*Jeb—Life is good, and this might be a perfect day
for a swim*

wishing that he were
elsewhere, preferably
near the water and
unconfined. On
meeting the visitors,
he raised his paw in
greeting and tilted his
head sadly to empha-
size his discontent.
Unable to resist the
big friendly dog,
the visitors started
adoption procedures
on the spot. The
next day, he was on
his way to Lake
Lashaway, Mass-
achusetts, with a new
name—"Jeb."

The first day home with Jeb was difficult, to put it mildly. First, from inside the house, he ripped the cat door out with his teeth. It took him only about ten seconds. Once outside he caught his collar on a hanging basket brought home from Maine that had not yet been hung. After that, the plant was in pieces, of course. Then the new owners' twelve-year-old Coon cat attacked Jeb, whereupon Jeb turned on their younger tiger cat, giving it such a scare that it took a good two or three years for them to accept each other. For a change of scene he was taken for a run in a 100-acre gravel pit, whereupon he had to be restrained (his new human "brother" had to lie down on top of him to restrain him). He had become so excited upon seeing another dog that he put his nose under the smaller dog and tossed him into the air. After this very first day with Jeb, the new owners were tempted to call the shelter to say that he was being returned. But they decided to give him more time. It paid off.

Jeb spent the rest of his life by the shore of the lake, having fun on early morning runs, retrieving pine cones and golf balls, swimming and acting as first mate to the captain in the big yellow motorboat. Water skiing became his favorite spectator sport, and his enthusiasm compelled him to dive right into the water to try to keep up with the skiers.

There were trips to Cape Cod Bay where he and his friends fished and cruised up and down the Cape Cod Canal. Only once was there trouble for Jeb on the Cape. He was intrigued to discover that skunks abound on the beach at night. One sprayed him liberally, and all the tomato juice on Cape Cod didn't help—especially when it started to rain. But best friends don't desert you in times of trouble; so Jeb rode back to Lake Lashaway with all the car windows open and endured a week of daily shampooing before the odor was gone.

As the blazing colors of autumn faded around the lake, winter winds began to howl, and the lake was frozen over. There was little fun to be had for a swimming dog and his friends; so a trip to a Florida beach was organized. Once again Jeb was walking by the Atlantic

*Boating anyone?*

Ocean, all the while remembering Penobscot Bay and Cape Cod.

On vacation, with time to kill until summer, Jeb quickly cultivated a new hobby. On morning walks by the tennis courts he began retrieving tennis balls, diving into the bushes and emerging sometimes with two balls at once. This really took some doing as well as a very big mouth. When spring began to make itself felt in the Northeast, Jeb and his family began the long trip home with his vacation souvenirs—19 tennis balls.

Back home to a cold rainy spring, Jeb helped out by trotting down the small peninsula to the road, where he met the mailman and delivered the mail back to the house himself. Jeb liked to participate directly in all his friends' activities. Soon it was golf season, and golf shots were practiced in the yard. But the balls had a perplexing way of disappearing, one by one. The mystery was solved one day as the lawn was being mowed. Behind the garden shed, his friends discovered Jeb's cache of golf balls.

It wasn't only golf balls behind that garden shed. When Jeb was especially fond of house guests, he would steal into their rooms, grab one of their socks and add them to his collection of favorite things behind the shed.

On weekends there were games of checkers to be played with friends. One player was very young, the other a grandfather, but Jeb held his own, moving checkers gently with his nose, making sure to move only his own men. Although he was a very large dog, he played gently with a two-year-old friend by dropping one of his tennis balls at the little boy's feet and waiting patiently for it to be thrown for him to retrieve.

From time to time there would be trips back to Penobscot Bay for Jeb and his friends, who were always made welcome at the Seven Mountains Motel in Camden as well as the Trade Winds Motor Inn in Rockland. There, on one occasion, Jeb slipped away from the room and was found by the door in the lobby, acting as a self-appointed greeter.

Last fall when a hurricane blew over Lake Lashaway, the big yellow boat had to come out of the water. Aware that the tremendous waves would make the job a difficult one, Jeb was put in the house while his friend, the skipper, took on the task alone. Reaching the boat ramp, the captain had just managed to float the boat onto the trailer when, suddenly, he caught sight of a large yellow head making its way toward him through the rough water. The first mate had broken through a storm door and swum the distance to the boat ramp to assist. After all, captain and crew support each other during difficult times, don't they?

Late last year (1999), we lost our Jeb to a sudden illness. He was everybody's friend, and we miss him terribly. Perhaps that's why we finally decided upon a name for the big yellow boat. It had been without a name for years, but this past summer (2000), our first without our

loyal companion, we continued to remember the water dog who loved the boat as much as we did and was always aboard when it left the shore. It is now *The Jeb*.

Our hope is that retired people will real-

*Jeb in his boat*

ize how rewarding it is to have pets when they have time for them. Being pack animals, it seems that dogs hate being alone. We doubt that Jeb would have done all of the surprising things he did if he had been left on his own all day. We're so glad we gave ourselves more time with him after that first traumatic day.

≈≈≈

Mary Morrissey lives with her husband as well as the legendary Ace (Labrador Retriever) and her thirteen-year-old cat Gulliver, who used to like to travel but now prefers to lie in a sunny window to watch the birds fly by.

In her job as manager of an apartment complex, Mary has found it appalling to discover how many unwanted cats and kittens are dumped in the apartment community, expected to forage for food in the dumpsters, and huddle by the laundry room under the drier vents for warmth during bad weather. With the help of Have-a-Heart traps, a nearby shelter, and some kind people, many of these cats have been saved. With local ads about spaying and neutering assistance, Mary hopes this practice of dumping unwanted pets can be ended.

During their years together Mary and her husband have taken in many cats and kittens and have provided foster care for others. They offer no fewer than 30 original and inspired names they have created for them. At the time of this writing, there are probably even more.

## HEROINES AMONG US

≋

### By Mary B. Morrissey
#### North Brookfield, Massachusetts

Some heroines are members of the cat family. One that comes to mind is a brave little tortie (tortoiseshell) living in a well-established community of perhaps 40 other feral cats. She may have been dumped there by an irresponsible person, as most of the others were.

Although this group is clustered around a working marina near sport fishing boats on Key Biscayne, it is still a hard life for the cats in their constant quest for food. The fishing boats have been known to share their bounty with the pelicans but not with the cats.

On this Florida island, there are good people who have noticed their struggle. Trying to make life a bit easier for the cats, these persons have formed a group, taking turns providing fresh water and dry cat food in a rainproof feeding station. A nearby veterinarian has offered her services; so whenever possible, newcomers to the feral group are apprehended and taken for spaying or neutering, then returned to the Marina. Some of the cats cannot be caught or handled, and the beautiful, wily tortie of which I write was one of those.

When it was time for her kittens to be born, she was hard-pressed to find a safe place for the event. There were a number of luxury yachts in the nearby boat slips, and she apparently noticed one in particular that was seldom moved or taken out on the water.

It was perfect, although it was a bit hard to make the jump over water into the boat with a belly full of kittens. But she managed, and in one of the long side pockets on the boat deck, she delivered four kittens. She cared for them well and after a few weeks decided it was time to move on. Hopping from the boat onto the dock with a kitten in her mouth was a bit tiring, but she managed to get them all safely ashore.

She found another boat that seemed suitable and was not quite so difficult to get into. She settled in with her family, and in no time at all, it seemed, the kittens grew and became quite rowdy. Once again, it was time to move them before they fell overboard during one of their wild wrestling bouts.

Just as the tortie took the last of the kittens ashore, a volunteer happened by who quickly apprehended all four and took them to a no-kill shelter for placement in homes with responsible owners.

It was only after the kittens were gone that the tortoiseshell mother allowed herself to be picked up and taken to the vet for spaying. Now she's back and getting a well-deserved rest. After all, motherhood can be exhausting. Under the circumstances of her life, her efforts seemed heroic.

*Homes would be nice, but at least the climate is temperate*

Mary Morrissey's biographical sketch is shown following *Jeb's Story*.

# THE ACE OF HEARTS LEARNS TO SWIM

≈

### By Mary B. Morrissey
#### North Brookfield, Massachusetts

O nce upon a time there was a wombat named **Ace**—or was he really a crazy, energetic pup? Here is his picture; so you can judge for yourself. He looked like a pup, but behaved like a tornado with sharp teeth. Maybe he isn't a puppy at all but one of those strange animals called "wombats" that resemble small bears.

*Ace—innocent puppy*
*Anyone need a good document shredder?*

Puppies are such fun, we thought. So we brought him home, and our life of never-ending vigilance started. Also, the destruction of personal property began as this small furry creature raced through our home on his own "search-and-destroy"missions.

But it was great fun watching this small ball of fur learn to swim and learn to love the water. It all began when I was trying to trim the bushes along our shoreline. Never has there been a bigger pest than Ace, as he kept biting at the clippers, trampling the day lilies, and biting the blossoms off the Black Eyed Susans that we had planted so carefully. It was vexing. Finally, in desperation to put a little space between us, I stepped into the water and swam away.

At a safe distance, I turned to see this plucky little four-month-old pup make friends with the water. Front legs in—back legs in—wade out a little bit—move all four legs at once—and he was swimming! Was it my imagination, or did a look of surprised pleasure appear as he swam toward me? I applauded his courage and resolve, while my daughter later noted how cute he looked in the water "with his ears floating like pontoons."

From that warm day on, he was at home in the water, and frequent swims were the order of the day for Ace. Summer days became fall days, and icy water temperatures did not seem to bother our fast-growing Ace. We shivered while we watched as he joyfully bounced into the water, ignoring the chill of icy water splashing against that bare puppy belly.

Will the kitchen floor ever be clean again, I wondered? Muddy paw prints were ever present. Mop them up and in he would come again after still another dip in the lake. Evidence was everywhere of a swimming and teething pup.

Why do the legs of your kitchen table appear to be stained red, our visitors asked? Why do your kitchen chairs look like they've been nibbled on? Why do you keep your shoes in the bookcase, and why are your many pairs of reading glasses piled up on a shelf six feet high?

Aha! Can't you guess? The table legs were painted with hot sauce to discourage the chewing pup. To our surprise, Ace loved the taste of hot sauce, so that was wasted effort. Only vigilance on our part kept the kitchen chairs standing, although the tooth marks will be there for some time to come.

When one is a frequent and enthusiastic swimmer, a big appetite is the result of all that activity in the fresh air. We watched in horror as a nylon knee stocking went "down the hatch" before we could take it from him. But not to worry, everything will come out all right, we thought as he raced into the kitchen and wolfed down a stolen stick of margarine from the kitchen counter (and it did).

Ace is a year old now, with permanent teeth in place, and we remember that popular song of a few years back, "I'll Walk Alone." Because of Ace, we won't have to walk alone or swim alone, either.

*Ace, sinking his teeth into the soft lining of the boat rail*

≋

Mary Morrissey's biographical sketch is shown following *Jeb's Story*.

# FIERCE TINA

≋

## By Meg Hunter
### Northport, Maine

Among all of our pets, Tina is the water lover. She's also the only one to come to us from a breeder. Our others were rescued as strays.

Pepé's rescue, for example, was dramatic. As my husband Charlie was driving his small truck along a busy Long Beach area street, he saw a small Apricot Poodle running madly along the road. He slowed, opened the truck door, and the dog jumped in. Charlie brought the dog home and begged me to take him in.

But I hesitated. At that point we already had Frisco and Dixie, and an elderly Yorkie named Sophie, who was near death.

Frisco is a black dog, said to be a mix of standard Schnauzer and Labrador. As a puppy, he was given to my husband by a woman in California who was not allowed to have pets in her apartment. About nine years old now and medium sized, Frisco has one blue eye and one brown. When clipped, he looks very "Schnauzery." Once quite mean, he now has space to run and has mellowed nicely.

Dixie is an elderly Seal Point Siamese my husband found when he worked for the city of Long Beach. She was a stray kitten living on the seashore until he rescued her.

So, for a while, I resisted taking in yet another stray. I called the local animal shelter to report finding a small Apricot Poodle (they didn't want to know). Then we had him washed and checked by a veterinarian. The dog was beautiful! The top of his head was without its usual pompom. He must have worn it away by rubbing against something. He loved children and, because we thought he came from a Spanish-speaking family, we called him "Pepé." He was a deep apricot color and very thin when he came to us. He had obviously been a pet that maybe got out and ran off, frightened by something. He was certainly terrified when my husband rescued him. Needless to say, we kept him, and he was a wonderful pet until we lost him to leukemia.

After our dear Pepé died, I searched for another dog. I looked in all the local shelters but finally realized that I wanted a puppy, not a full-grown dog. I had admired Jack Russell Terriers for a while and had had two Yorkshire Terriers previously. Both were little clowns and great company, so I knew I related to terrier temperament as though I had once been one! Following advice from a local shelter, I contacted a highly recommended breeder of Jack Russell Terriers and found Tina. Her birthday is October 4, three days before mine—both Librans. She had a different name when I bought her at five months of age, but I took one look at her strutting walk—just like Tina Turner—and named her "Tina."

When Tina came to live with us, it took some time for her to adjust and begin exploring our property in Northport. After a few months, she became comfortable with her surroundings. She discovered the stream that feeds the pond behind our house and flows on to the seashore beyond. The pond is fed by a tumbling flow of water that sounds like an avalanche when in full spate. There's a small waterfall that crashes into a shallow pool before flowing under the bridge and into the pond.

Tina started dashing across the bridge and throwing herself into the "white water" as it came into the paddling pool, snapping at the torrent and trying to catch it. Then she would

*Tina – on the alert as she surveys her world*

come out, shake herself and go back in again. Even when fall turned to winter and ice began to form, she continued to run into the icy stream until I was afraid she would freeze her muscular little legs. Finally, just before Christmas, when the ice had completely covered the surface and we could just see the water flowing sluggishly underneath, Tina admitted her game was over until the spring.

*Tina attacking the "white water" in the stream.*

It always amazed me that she plays with the water the way she does, because she showed no interest in the pond. In fact, she was desperate to get out of the water once when she slipped off the bank and fell in. But Jack Russells are aggressive little dogs, and I believe Tina wants to subdue the moving water and make it stop. Whatever her reasons, this is her very favorite form of play, and it is always amusing to watch. Happily, she gets some great hydrotherapy while my husband and I benefit from this special form of pet therapy.

Tina is a very loving dog, passionate about everything she does, whether playing with her companion, Frisco (who still lives with us) or chasing a tossed ball or tugging fiercely on her knotted rope pull-toy.

She can be very aggressive and growls whenever she doesn't like something. But she is friendly and has always won praise at the veterinarian's for her lack of bad temper.

We are so glad to have her in our lives.

≋

Margaret (Meg) Sharp Hunter was born in Croydon, England. Her husband Charles is from Glasgow, Scotland. Her path to Midcoast Maine was a circuitous one that, through many adventures, took her to Melbourne, Australia, to Montreal, Canada, to Camden for fifteen years, then on to California where she met and married Charlie. After nine years on the West Coast and following the Northridge earthquake in 1993, Meg persuaded her husband to return with her to Maine "where the earth doesn't shift so much." They moved with their beloved pets in 1994 and found the perfect spot to settle—on 42 acres in Northport, in an old house built in 1797—the Carver Homestead— which used to be a stagecoach stop, then a boarding house for travelers from the islands who worked on the mainland.

Both Meg and her husband have had diverse work experience, but at the time of this writing she is Executive Assistant to the Director of Kno-Wal-Lin Home Care in Rockland. He is a broker at Jaret & Cohn Real Estate, Belfast office. They also have diverse interests—she is a vintage car enthusiast and auto racing fan—he, an actor with the Belfast Maskers (civic theater) and an avid soccer fan.

Meg says that "with the sea almost at our front door and moose, owls, ferrets, deer, eagles, even coyotes, almost in our back yard, we are very content here in Midcoast Maine."

## ABBY AND A.J.—GREAT RETRIEVERS

≋

### By Robin L. Chapman
*Thomaston, Maine*

This story is about my two Golden Retrievers, Abby and A.J. Throughout my years with the dogs, they have become inseparable and travel with me most everywhere in my truck—Abby beside me and A.J. by the window. Family and friends often see us on our way to Dairy Queen for ice cream cones—vanilla soft-serve preferred.

Others know of Abby and A.J. too, because in September of 1997 a local newspaper, the *Courier-Gazette* of Rockland, Maine, wrote a story about the dogs, describing their outstanding skills as retrievers, with their loot in the form of softballs.

Abby and A.J. always attended the games in which I played during the Elks Businessmen's Softball League season. On their own, they brought back to the bench the softballs that were hit into the woods

*A.J. (left) with Abby*

behind the fence. It made no difference when the balls were lost—old or new—they were retrieved by this talented duo. By the end of the season more than 40 softballs had been collected. They were then donated to the Thomaston Recreation Program. Abby and A.J. became local heroes for their prowess in this field of endeavor.

Without a doubt, however, the most enjoyable thing on the dogs' "to-do" list is swimming and retrieving rocks from the lake bottom. A.J. does OK in the shallows, but Abby is the master. She will dive in deeper water for up to fifteen seconds and usually come up with a rock. I always wondered whether or not she feels for them or keeps her eyes open to find them. To satisfy my curiosity, I took an underwater photograph to learn the answer (See the accompanying picture). No question—she keeps her eyes open.

This wonderful dog was a puppy when I got her in May of 1991. She came from a litter of six and was what I call a calendar puppy. She had all the traits of a Golden—big feet, cute wrinkly nose, and soft, sandy, fluffy hair. She grew very quickly and took to the water from the

*Abby, eyes open, retrieving rocks from the lake bottom*

start. I made sure to train her in some basic skills: sit, stay, and lay as well as the important ones like staying out of the road and not jumping out of the car until allowed.

A.J. came into my life in 1995 at an age of about eight years. My daughter Wendy got him from an abusive home and couldn't keep him in her apartment; so she asked me if I would take him in. After a few days, he started to fit in and has been a part of the family ever since.

The happiness these two dogs have given me is immeasurable. Their warm, tail-wagging welcomes are a joy to come home to after a long day at work. Anyone thinking about getting a dog should consider a pair. They are twice the fun and truly man's best friend.

≋

Robin Chapman was born and raised in Midcoast Maine. He attended local schools and graduated from Medomak Valley High School. In 1980 he joined the U.S. Navy for four years, seeing much of the Pacific Coast and many Asian countries. Returning to Maine in 1986, he lived and worked in the Portland area. In 1989 he trained in Texas to be a commercial diver and worked in that field for seven years. Abby and A.J. have a central role in his life, but Robin also enjoys boating, fishing, golf, skiing, and travel. He works as a correctional officer at the Maine State Prison in Warren and resides in Thomaston with his dogs.

# AGROUND IN NANTUCKET WITH THE GIRLS

### By Virginia Biddle, M.D.
#### Blue Hill, Maine

I was living in Woods Hole at the time, and my boat was the 29-foot yawl named *Saga*. A friend and I had planned an overnight escape to Nantucket, way up behind the outer barrier sand bars, the anchorage for which is reached by a serpentine, unbuoyed passage navigable only at high water. Our crew members were Yuri, a black German Shepherd and her niece Becka, whose mother had had an unplanned fling with a yellow Lab.

Yuri was a dignified, sensitive, and serious dog who had unhesitatingly assumed responsibility for helping to raise her 10 nieces and nephews, born in my cellar. Most of the litter looked like black Shepherds except for Becka, the lemon drop. She was a ridiculous, exuberant dog with short legs, a tubby blonde body, Shepherd nose and droopy ears. The other puppies sold fast, but Becka was too silly looking to sell, and, besides, she and Yuri were devoted to one another. They came to be known collectively as "The Girls."

The approach we made on our overnight escape was perfectly executed, dropping the hook just before sunset at high tide. We had walked the dogs on

*Becka and Yuri — "The Girls" in Vermont*

*At home in bed*

the beach, and it was time to break out the rum. Imagine our shock and horror to discover that the freshwater tank had surreptitiously emptied itself into the bilge leaving us without a drop of water. By then the tide had started to ebb, and the sun was beginning to sink. Without a second's hesitation we resolved to make a dash for it.

About half way through that winding channel I miscalculated by a few feet and ran *Saga* hard onto a sandbar. Nothing would induce her to budge, the tide was disappearing like water down a bathtub drain, and we began, ever so gently, to lie over on our side. Becka and Yuri, being nobody's fools, quickly repaired to the down side of the bunks where they remained comfortably immovable until we were able to kedge the boat off at 4 a.m. Having had almost no sleep, we felt cramped and disgruntled. The Girls, however, arose fresh, rested, and bemused at this latest adventure dreamed up by their mother for their entertainment.

≋≋≋

Virginia Biddle was born in Milton, Massachusetts, and, she says, "grew up largely on the back of a horse when not surviving on-going attempts at formal education." Something of a maverick, she went through an abortive stint in a degree nursing program, became a registered medical technologist, and spent two years in Nagasaki, Japan, as medical director of a research laboratory for the Atomic Bomb Casualty Commission. Later, after entering medical school at the age of thirty-one, Dr. Biddle received her medical degree from Columbia University College of Physicians and Surgeons. She opened her own practice in Falmouth, Massachusetts, on Cape Cod and enjoyed what she considers to be the last really good years in medicine before HMOs and other regulatory agencies "started drowning us all in meaningless, redundant paper work." With regret, she closed her practice and moved to Maine, where she has worked for a walk-in clinic and accepted some *locum tenens* assignments in various states. She gardens, hauls lobster pots, sails (with a captain's license), skis, "builds things" and is currently assisted by two cats and her cozy, affectionate Wolf-dog, Josie.

# BELLA—PART WOLF, ALL LOVE

≋

## By *Virginia Biddle, M.D.*
### *Blue Hill, Maine*

Bella was born in Falmouth, Massachusetts, and moved to Maine ten years ago when she was two. Her mother was a German Shepherd who had eleven pups by a half-wolf dog from Maine. I never met the father, but Bella's mother was a sweet dog who allowed me into the pen with all of her beautiful babies. When I tried to select one of them to adopt, I learned that my first two choices were spoken for. I decided to take the runt, who became "Bella." Luckily, I picked her up sooner than planned at just five weeks of age. I say, "luckily," because the entire remaining litter was stolen shortly thereafter while the owners were at work.

*Nikko guarding his dog*

Bella came home to begin her education with me and my wise old male cat Nikko, who had already "brought up" three previous dogs. One day I looked out the window to behold Bella sitting on Nikko, peering over her shoulder to see how he was taking it. When I rushed to the rescue, I discovered that Nikko was purring!

From early on Bella showed a strong aptitude for boats and the water. She follows me unhesitatingly into any boat, no matter how

*Bella waiting to go haul traps*

unlikely it might appear, and knows just how to behave. She learned quickly that I need her in the bow of the skiff to balance my weight in the stern and so perches herself like a figurehead, with buttocks on the seat and front feet on the floor like a person.

While lobstering with me Bella attends each haul with deep interest, moaning in anticipation as each pot comes aboard. She yelps appreciatively for lobster, barks disapprovingly at crabs, and a red nun buoy too close at hand evokes a fit of disciplinary barking.

Bella adores the water, swims at any time of the year, among ice flows if necessary, and loves nothing more than to fetch a thrown stick, leaving a wake like a motorboat. She goes everywhere with me and seduces people in droves, from Alaska to Florida. When she disappears on boating picnics, I have only to look down the beach to find her with another group, having conned someone into throwing something for her. Several people have told me in complete seriousness that Bella had winked at them.

Bella has an indefatigable desire and ability to catch Frisbees and retrieve

*A thrown stick would be nice*

anything thrown. Weeds tossed from the garden produce a near frenzy of leaping and chasing, and nothing delights her more than a shovel full of snow right in the face.

*Nikko with Bella—so warm—so safe—together*

But for all the playing, Bella is a deeply intelligent and sensitive dog who knows exactly what is expected of her in any situation. She comes to work with me when I spend ten-hour days at the clinic. There, I often find her holding court to ecstatic two-year-olds, or little old ladies leaning down, making cooing noises. Patients come as much to see Bella as to get my medicines.

When I'm working outdoors, and Bella is plaguing me to throw a stick, I sometimes order her to "Go play by yourself; I'm busy!" She disappears into the woods, and soon I hear piteous squealing noises. Bella has found a large rock and is dragging it backwards between her front paws, talking to it. She is playing by herself. She understands English to an uncanny degree, so that people often resort to spelling words around her.

Bella adores old cat Nikko, who washes her face, cleans her ears, and sleeps right up against her whenever he can.

About a year ago Bella began to limp with one hind leg. Soon that foot was dragging to the point that she has to wear a leather boot to keep from abrading all the skin from the top of her foot. She has to be helped upstairs but is furious with me for building a ramp to the deck. She absolutely will not use it.

*Rival Deucy making Nikko jealous*

Bella has an arthritic old Lab friend and neighbor who adores her. They stagger off together to do their business on each other's lawns. Yesterday we all hobbled down to the shore, and the two old dogs repaired blissfully into the ocean. Bella ferociously shook her stick while her friend, Jake, just lay in the water smiling.

Things take longer and occur with much less vigor, but they do happen, and at least for a time, wise old cat Nikko enjoyed his retirement. Then Bella found a tiny abandoned kitten in the garden; so now Nikko has rival "Deucy" to disapprove of and complain to me about. But there'll be no new dogs to raise just yet.

## EPILOGUE

Bella's condition worsened. A Wyoming veterinarian tried a series of acupuncture treatments to no avail. When both hind legs gave out, she was taken to an animal neurologist in Portland, Maine, who did a myelogram and diagnosed a progressive degenerative process much like ALS or Lou Gehrig's disease. I learned of wheels for paralyzed dogs and ordered a custom set. When the time came to use them, Bella was enthusiastic and mobile again. She became a familiar sight at the Yacht Club, barreling down the gangway in her wheelchair. She could swim long after she could no longer walk. Then last spring her front legs began to fail, and she was unable to support the wheels. We spent a quiet time together under the apple tree before a final visit to the veterinarian, where she died in my arms.

On that very day Josie, nearly two-thirds wolf and one-third Malamute with a dash of Shepherd thrown in, was born and came home with me nine weeks later. Old cat Nikko is now bringing up his fourth dog.

*Bella with her wheels; the author in a cast and on crutches following an ankle injury — "Two old cripples in a tug of war"*

Dr. Biddle's biographical sketch is shown following the story, *Aground in Nantucket with The Girls.*

# JOSIE

### By Virginia Biddle, M.D.
#### Blue Hill, Maine

Josie is helpful in ways that would have horrified Bella. Josie has a somewhat looser code of ethics, which goes something like this: When your mother has just finished planting bulbs and carefully covered them with mulch, go dig up a few and move them to a more appropriate place, say under the pine tree, where you buried your last bone. Then triumphantly bring her one so she'll see just how useful you've been. When she addresses you in rude and unflattering terms, look confused and hurt so she'll forget how awful you are and hug you. If you should find your mother working in the perennial bed, jump over the fence (which is designed to keep you out), sit firmly on a delphinium and lean affectionately against her legs, thereby pinning her to the stone wall as you chew meditatively on the handle of her shovel. If your mother persists in doing these boring chores instead of taking you for a walk, try stealing a roll of the plastic twine that goes in the weed-whacker, chew it into six-inch lengths, being sure to eat a few so you can throw them up later on the bedroom rug along with the cat's dinner you filched earlier.

Josie knows perfectly well that she's beautiful and that I adore her. In the early morning when I first let her out, she flies across the field into the slanty autumn sun and all the silvery tips of her long, white coat quiver and shimmer like an expensive animated halo. When her girlfriend Bonnie comes to visit, they fall into each other's arms and roll around on the lawn in mock battle. Lips drawn back, teeth bared, they sing into each other's faces, one soprano and the other alto. Then they leap on and off the lobster float in a version of "I'm the king of the castle...."

I wish Josie were happier in boats. She swims year 'round with great glee, but pitching about on top of the water makes her nervous. She paces from one end of the boat to the other, panting and threatening to fall overboard at any moment. Once back on land she is in her element and a joy to take for a walk. She bolts off into the woods, big grin on her face, tail waving, and disappears. Just as I'm sure she's gone

*Josie, watching carefully to see how she can "help"*

for good and probably half-way to Bangor, Josie materializes beside me, smiling reassuringly as if to say, "Don't worry, Mom, I won't leave you!"

Like Bella, Josie is a good traveler and a civilized visitor. First of all, she prefers to be outdoors; so she doesn't expect to be included in cocktails and dinner. When she does agree to come in, she greets everyone politely and then retreats quietly to the guest room and goes to sleep with her head on my coat.

Now, lest you are beginning to think that Josie is a perfect dog, I must tell you that she is also a consummate thief: gloves, eyeglasses, pills, cameras, anything plastic. The trouble is that I can't stay mad at her for long. We have endless and useless talks about her bad behavior, and I end up with my arms around her while she looks sanctimonious.

≋

Dr. Biddle's biographical sketch is shown following the story entitled, *Aground in Nantucket with The Girls.*

# FROM FEAR TO LOVE

≋

*By Evelyn M. Boyington*
*Rockland, Maine*

When I was growing up we had cats from time to time but never a family dog. And my experiences with dogs outside the home were not positive ones.

First, I saw the German Shepherd next door bite a girl from across the street. From then on, every time that dog barked, I was so scared I'd go around to the other side of our house to play.

Then when I was about nine years old, out riding my bike, a large dog bit me on the leg and knocked me down. The wounds weren't deep, but after that I was terrified of all dogs. Whenever I got near one, I could feel goose bumps, and the hair on my arms would rise.

But later, when I was married and living on a farm in Mars Hill, Maine, my husband wanted to get a dog for the children to play with. I finally agreed, and he brought home a small ball of black-and-white fur the children named "Lady." How could anyone be afraid of a loving, trusting puppy?

Lady was a very gentle dog and wonderful with the children. When she was young they dressed her up and took her for rides in the doll carriage or in their little red wagon. They played ball with her and ran all over the yard playing tag and chasing her. She followed them wherever they went.

As Lady grew older, she began exploring the neighborhood. Some people up the road took a liking to her and started giving her treats. They were happy to keep her for a week while we were on vacation. After that, she spent more and more time there. Eventually we let those neighbors keep her, but we all missed her after she became their dog instead of ours.

When we moved to Rockland, we got a puppy that we named

"Peezer" in memory of a dog my husband had as a child. Peezer had a real hang-up with the postman and mail delivery because of a leather strap swung at him by the mail carrier. Every day was a struggle to protect both Peezer and the postman and to retrieve the mail from the mail slot before Peezer could grab it and make tooth marks all over it.

We had Peezer for about seven years before he broke loose from his tether, ran out into the road, and was killed by a passing car. As difficult as he was in relation to mail delivery, we missed him for all of his other endearing qualities—and there were many.

Our next dog, a black Labrador Retriever named Tony, was the pet who really captured my heart.

He'd get into mischief—the cat food, for instance. With one or two swipes of his tongue all the food in the cat's dish would disappear. So I put the bowl on the kitchen stool where the cat could eat in peace and later, as Tony grew, in other even higher safe places.

My son John would take Tony along on his early morning paper route. In my mind's eye, I can still see the two of them (Tony almost as big as John by then) trudging home, covered with snow. One time John harnessed Tony to the sled on which he hauled his papers. Tony went dashing off into people's yards, spilling papers all over the road.

On Saturdays John would usually take Tony with him when he went to his father's service station. During the summer, Tony loved to take off from the back of the garage and go down along the waterfront, where he enjoyed exploring the shore.

A fish plant that made mother-of-pearl was operating there at that time. Without the types of controls in place today, there were fish heads, tails, and body parts strewn along the beach, and Tony figured that was a good place for lunch. When he returned to the garage, wet and reeking of dead fish, he would go over to the hose and stand there, shivering, waiting for John to wash him off. Evidently the stench was so bad even Tony couldn't stand it!

The men at the garage always had Coca Cola to drink. But if a bottle had been left upright on the floor, Tony would carry it around in his mouth. When he tired of toting it, he would lay it on its side on the floor so the liquid would spill out and he could lap it up.

When the weather was hot, John and his sister Alice would head for Chickawaukie Lake after work—with Tony riding in the back of the pick-up. All would plunge in for a swim. Tony loved swimming so much he would stay in the water all the time they were there and refuse to hop into the truck when it was time to come home. Instead, tongue hanging out, he ran behind it all the way back. He would be dry by the time he had run the mile home.

*Tony—well-loved and ready to play*

It was impossible to keep Tony tied in the dooryard. He would break every rope or chain with which we tried to fetter him. We had to try, though, because of Rockland's leash law.

One day Tony broke loose and went bounding down the road, glad to be free. Some neighbors said he had bothered the pet lamb they had tied behind their house. At this point we decided it was best to give Tony to some people who owned a farm where he could roam the fields without having to be tethered or on a leash. He had become so much a part of our lives, though, it was heart-wrenching for all of us the day they took Tony away to his new home.

Looking back, I can see that by having our own dogs to nurture and enjoy, my fears and dread were transformed first into tolerance, then into affection, and, finally, into love. Our pets will always have a special place in my heart.

≈≈

Evelyn M. Boyington was born and raised in New York but has lived in Maine most of her life. Following her graduation from college and throughout her married life she was a teacher of music, especially piano. She is a "puzzle buff" and has had many of her puzzles published by *Penny Press* magazine. She co-authored *Down East Puzzles and Word Games* and is the sole author of *Bible Crosswords #12*, published by Barbour, Inc. The mother of four children, she has numerous grandchildren and great-grandchildren. Her love of pets continues, and she says it is hard to remember a time when her family was without them.

≈≈≈≈≈

Mrs. Boyington passed away before this book reached print.

# MAMA DUCK—A MOTHER'S SENSE

## By Christa Richardson
### Martha's Vineyard, Massachusetts

People have said that I have a "special connection" with animals. They describe it as a gift—a quality that allows me uncommon access into the animals' world. Not so. I just have a willingness to communicate on whatever level is possible. The information is always there—like the hidden illustration in a child's book. The drawing is easy for children to locate, because they are willing to look.

Tom and I lived in a condominium in Alexandria, Virginia. Our home was in the busy, over-developed part of the city, crowded with condos, townhouses, convenience stores, and mini malls. There is little space there for wildlife beyond sparrows, crows, and squirrels.

Several years ago, in the middle of a warm, late-summer afternoon, we returned from a weekend trip. As we pulled into our parking spot near the pool, I noticed a female Mallard duck standing in a patch of grass in the corner. I commented to Tom on the unusual sight of a duck standing next to our parking lot. I sat in the car for a moment, expecting her to move on. She stood there on the grass patch. Tired from a long drive, we eventually unloaded the car and went inside.

I mentioned the duck to a housemate, and he said she'd been there all weekend. I went back outside to check and, as I walked to the pool, I asked each person I passed about the duck. "Oh, she's hungry, we've been feeding her like crazy." Everything a duck would normally gobble up lay scattered on the grass. I watched her for a few minutes. She was pacing, ignoring offerings of cereal, corn, and bits of bread. Her head was low and she was clearly worried about something.

There were no other ducks in sight, and I asked the neighbors if she had actually eaten any of the food or been in the pool. They weren't sure but kept throwing new food her way. Tom came outside,

*Mama duck pacing*

and we watched her for several minutes. She didn't shy away from people as they approached. She just kept pacing. She seemed tired but not injured, so after watching for several minutes more, Tom and I returned to our ground floor apartment to unpack.

Half an hour later we were stretched out for a nap. Our bedroom, in the corner of the building close to the pool, had a small window facing the parking lot. I was still thinking about the duck but couldn't imagine why she would wander around the pool area, without a mate or an appetite. Tom and I both fell asleep.

"Quack."

I opened my eyes.

"Quack."

That duck sounded really close.

"Quack quack."

KC, our normally oblivious dog, was on the bed, using Tom's shoulder to peer out the window. We both sat up (much easier for me without a wriggling 60-pound dog!) and listened.

"Quack quack quack"

No doubt about it, she was right under the bedroom window. She delivered a hoarse but determined final quack.

Now KC had balanced herself on the slippery headboard of the bed and nosed the sliding glass open. We all looked out and down at the duck. She stood below the middle of our window. With it finally open, she tilted her head, looked me straight in the eye and, despite a barking dog, didn't budge. I retreated to pull on jeans and noticed Tom doing the same but more slowly. I was rushing, afraid the duck would leave before we could make it outside. Tom had seen that duck's look and knew better. We left KC in the bedroom and walked several yards in the opposite direction to the front door. I stepped out into the hallway and there was the duck.

We followed the duck, as asked. She walked confidently back toward the high grassy patch with me following, Tom next, and a small assortment of now-interested neighbors behind. I distinctly remember two blond-haired twins. They had no idea what was going on, but they were certain something interesting was happening. After all, it isn't every day a duck leads a procession of adults across a parking lot.

A young couple stood at the ready with more bread and said, "Oh, there she is. We brought her some fresh bread." I stopped at the edge of the parking lot and looked at the Mallard. "She can't get to her babies; that's what she needs help with."

The duck was standing several feet away from a storm drain. I walked over to it, leaned my head in under the concrete barrier, and put up a hand to ask the small crowd to be quiet. I heard nothing. I waited, and looked up at the duck. She had stopped pacing and sat, exhausted, in the grass.

After several minutes I could hear only a trickle of water and saw nothing but masses of rotting leaves. I was sure the ducklings were close but wondered how two days in this heat might have affected them. I asked Tom to listen at the next drain, several yards away and down the hill. We continued to listen, and a kind neighbor provided flashlights. Nothing. We checked two other storm drains, one above the original site where the duck stood and one across the street. There was absolutely no sign of ducklings; alive or otherwise.

Frustrated, I took a last look and went back with Tom into the apartment. Where was her mate? Maybe there were no ducklings and he had been hit by a car or killed by a feral cat in the nearby lot. We sat on the edge of the bed; Tom stretched out and fell asleep. I joined him.

"Quack quack."

Now I knew that duck wasn't interested in my doubt or fatigue. I also knew she didn't have time to spare! Tom headed straight for the storm drain over which Mama Duck had paced all weekend. He stuck his head far into the opening. I went to the second drain, and we positioned ourselves again. I was beginning to wonder if the situation were hopeless, and I began to question whether or not we should move the duck. Then Tom yelled: "I hear them! I hear them!" I rushed up the hill and stuck my head down into the drain. Sure enough, tiny peeps could be heard from the darkest corner of the leaf- and debris-covered drain. Someone handed me a flashlight, and there they were! Four tiny, trembling black and yellow babies huddled together in the leaves, trying to keep from slipping toward the moving water. I withdrew my head, and Mama Duck met me at the edge of the cement block.

"I was just about to give up," I told Tom as we ran inside for a phone and equipment. "They were saving their energy—barely able to make noise periodically," he reasoned.

From then on, it was a smooth ride. We called Alexandria Animal

*Kelvin and Tom—what to do?*

Rescue. They promised they would come as quickly as possible. I explained that the ducklings had been down there without food or water for at least sixty hours. We then called a couple of neighbors and put together a "duck fishing pole" consisting of a bucket on a thin rope. Tom and Kelvin, a neighbor, tried to drag the bucket toward the ducklings but they didn't understand. I wanted to wait for the local rescue van, fearing the bucket would send them farther into the storm drain or, worse yet, stumbling into the running water.

I still wondered what had happened to the male duck when I noticed Mama Duck running to take off. "Oh no ... all the people and commotion have scared her off," I thought. Then I realized she was circling the area, probably stretching her wings and possibly signaling the mate who may have been looking for help as well.

The rescue unit showed up less than an hour later and quickly lowered a net and pole into the drain. They pulled up four very tired ducklings. We all said hello to the little brood, wondering if they knew what a close call they had had! I held the four lucky ducklings in my hands and admired their complete lack of fear.

Mama Duck was still circling. On the advice of the experts, we placed the ducklings in the grass and moved back. She swooped down, lined them up and marched them to safety—Away from storm drains.

How could this mother from another species know which humans might be willing and able to help her? She came directly to our window—one among hundreds in the area. She apparently sensed our concern and was determined to make us understand her need to find and retrieve her lost babies. She was calling specifically to us.

The "gift" of understanding across species is available to every one of us. The secret? Respect for each creature, a willingness to listen, and certainly love—a great deal of it. With these basics in place, total honesty comes to the surface, and that is what animals respond to. If my intent is to do an animal no harm, that sincerity is recognized. I might be talking to a frightened animal in words, but she will accept my help because it is clear there is no threat. When our motivations are honest and good, communication comes more easily because guards are lowered. Animals know that when our actions are driven by such sincerity, their safety and freedom are not in jeopardy.

We are so glad Mama Duck recognized these conditions. She persisted and managed to tell us what we needed to know.

≈≈≈

Christa Richardson's dedication to all creatures began at an early age. It started when a tiny featherless bird was bumped out of its nest when she was just four years old. Many tears followed. The small creature didn't have the strength to survive, but a process had begun for that little girl. Soon squirrels, cats, dogs; any animal that needed a voice found one. The sentiment is even stronger today, and the animals have grown as well. Horses, along with other animals, have made themselves heard and found care and love in her hands.

A continuing battle with the serious illness CFIDS (Chronic Fatigue Immune Dysfunction Syndrome) has reduced the author's capacity for horseback riding and physical work but not the love and interest she shows. Patiently watching the interactions and behavior of animals is crucial to understanding their past. Only then, she says, can they be given a future. And this is the author's promise to the animals she meets.

# FUZZY—WHO SAW THE SEA

## By Stephanie Clapp
### Cellardoor Winery, Lincolnville, Maine

Fuzzy was captain of all that he could see, and he saw the sea.

This is the story of a very special cat. We knew this was an important cat the minute we saw him at the Camden-Rockport Animal Shelter in December 1986.

We told the lady at the desk we were looking for a boat cat. She looked at us and sized up the situation. She quizzed us on the type of boat, where we were going, how far, how fast, and what experience we had. She told us they did not like to let cats go to people on boats, because, in so many words, boat people could be questionable caretakers and boats could be problematic environments for pets. We pleaded our case with great conviction; this was the cat we wanted! After about an hour of going back and forth, she said that if we promised that

Prancer was secured below deck while we were under way, she would let us take him. We were jubilant! We had the smartest and handsomest cat in the place.

We went back to our boat, an 85-foot ketch, and introduced them to each other. The first day it became obvious that the cat's name did not

*Fuzzy with a fishy treat next to the storm anchor of the* Windermere

work for us. We tried many names over the next week, but we kept calling him "fuzzy cat." We couldn't think of anything better; so "Fuzzy" became his name.

Fuzzy learned to walk the boom, jump from house to deck and climb in the rigging. He could fly around the outside railing. The rail was only six inches wide, but that was all he needed. He loved his boat and everyone who came near it. We taught him to sit in the saloon while we were underway. He knew that when the harness and leash came out we were going to move on to the next harbor. He accepted this as the price of freedom.

Fuzzy did fall overboard several times. The first time it was February and cold. We were tied up to the dock, and he went up on deck. Next thing I heard was a splash. He had slipped on the ice and fallen eight feet into the water. Fuzzy swam to the icy shore as I climbed down under the dock to save him. I slipped and slid but eventually succeeded in getting him. When I finally had him on the boat, he ran down the companionway and into the bathroom. Yes, bathroom. He hopped into the tub and waited for me to rinse him off with fresh warm water—something familiar to him, because he enjoyed warm baths (really!).

One other notable swim occurred when he saw an "island" of foam and seaweed float by and mistook it for solid land. This time, it was summer and not too cold. He swam back to the boat and was able to climb out of the water and up the ladder.

We rarely tied up to land; so Fuzzy didn't go ashore much. On one outing, though, my husband was rowing Fuz to an island so he could run in the grass. But Fuz decided he did not want to leave his boat and jumped over the side. He swam back, paddling as fast and as high out of the water as he could. He managed to get on board by himself this time too.

We have sold the boat and moved many times in the past twelve years. Fuzzy adjusts well to all of our moves. He has been a boat cat, a

*Fuzzy on land and at rest near his water*
*fountain—dreaming of the sea, perhaps?*

beach cat, a city cat, an inn cat and now a country cat. He has seen the
world and ended up right back home. He is sitting in my lap as I write
these notes, no doubt waiting for his next adventure. Meanwhile, his
new world includes a farm with built-in outdoor enclosure with ramp
and cat door. He is now the great hunter, with fond memories of being
a fisherman.

Thanks, CRARL, for the best cat.

≈

Stephanie Clapp and her husband John adopted Fuzzy after having
sold the Granite Inn in Rockland and moved onto their 85-foot
historic sailboat, the *Windermere*, a Baltic Trader they rebuilt in
Rockland harbor. They later sold the boat, moved to Savannah,
Georgia, where they found their second cat, Shrimpy—an abandoned
kitten with a taste for shrimp. A subsequent move back to Maine
brought them full-circle. They bought the Inn again, redecorated, and
were back in business until the country called. The Inn was sold in

1997. The Clapps moved to a farm in Lincolnville and opened the Cellardoor Winery. When they decided to adopt a dog, off to the Camden-Rockport Shelter they went, and there he was—their new best friend—whose name became "Angus." With two rooms for farm-stay, Angus often gets to take walks with guests along the trails of Camden Hills State Park. "He's the greatest dog," Stephanie said, "but we love all of our pets, and now Fuzzy is old but, as of this writing, he is still the king of the hill."

*Shrimpy and Fuzzy—guess who's still in charge?*

*The following is a slightly revised version of a story that first appeared*
*in* Sail *magazine, Vol. 28, No. 10, October, 1997.*
*It is reproduced here courtesy of* Sail *with permission of the author.*

## LOVELY WAS A SAILOR

### By Joseph E. Brown
#### Rockport, Maine

She was only a cat, but in many ways she was probably the best crew we ever signed aboard our old cruising yawl, *Gracie.*

She was called "Lovely," although we cannot claim authorship of that name. It was given to her by her previous owner, Janet Sanso, who, in her typical English fashion when trying to decide on a name, exclaimed to herself, "Oh, what a lovely cat!" The name stuck.

Unlike most cats that instinctively fear the sea, Lovely reveled in being near, on, or sometimes even under salt water, having been raised at the marina where we lived aboard *Gracie* in San Diego Bay.

The day we met Janet, she was walking toward her car, carrying Lovely in a cat carrier, on her way to the local animal shelter. It seemed Janet's mother in England was seriously ill and Janet, who owned a pilot cutter at our marina, reluctantly was forced to give up both boat and cat. Lovely faced the prospect of six months in English quarantine, a distressing and costly prospect that Janet refused to consider.

My wife, Anne, and I, aware of the tremendous overpopulation of cats at the local shelter and being equally aware of how that population periodically was reduced, could not accept Lovely's pending fate. To Janet's great delight, we became Lovely's new owners—and so began a serendipitous relationship that would endure for nearly seventeen years.

Lovely adapted almost instantly to *Gracie*, during both the times we spent at the dock and the hours we were at sea. She was a born sea cat, no question about it. And no two-legged crew ever adjusted as quickly and as contentedly to a sea-going life as did our affectionate little brown tabby.

Despite her small size, she defended her turf with an intensity more suited to a tiger in the wild. More than once, I laughed out loud as Lovely, neck fur bristling in anger, chased an intruding cat or dog right off the dock and into the water, despite the fact that most were twice her size and many times as mean.

More than once Lovely had her own unscheduled dip in San Diego Bay, but, with one exception, she always managed to get out without help. The exception began about 2 a.m. on a frightfully cold night in March when Anne and I were awakened by a series of plaintive meows which, unmistakably, were those of our furry little crew. I went on deck, but no cat was in sight. The meowing was coming from under the wooden float to which *Gracie* was tied. Having fallen in, Lovely somehow had managed to crawl into an air space under the dock's wooden planks. Her only recourse would have been to swim back underwater to our boat, an option Lovely refused to consider.

To rescue her, I had only one course of action, and my body shivers even now when I recall what happened next that bitter winter night. Stripping to my shorts (I didn't own a wet suit) I dove into the blackened water, swam under the dock and surfaced in the air space where Lovely, shivering and yowling only moments before, gave me a welcome lick.

By now the reader must have guessed what followed. The only way back to the boat was to swim underwater once again, clutching Lovely tightly against my chest. When we reached safety, her claws had transformed my chest and arms into what looked like a bramble-scratched mess.

On another occasion, she had an even closer call. It began on a spring afternoon when Lovely was snoozing below as we began inching our way out of our slip under power. Our engine, a cantankerous gas model more than twenty-five years old, belched smoke like an erupting Vesuvius. Since we were backing into the wind, Lovely got the full brunt of its noxious fumes. Shaking herself awake, she decided she'd had enough; she'd go ashore.

As if yesterday, I can remember the blur of Lovely's body zipping past my face as I stood at the tiller. Then, discovering to her horror that water, not the familiar dock, lay directly below, she reversed herself in mid-air, caught her claws on *Gracie*'s appropriately-named toe rail, and finally struggled aboard. Shaking with the realization of almost having exhausted another one of her nine lives, Lovely then tippy-toed below, threw up her favorite Fancy Feast salmon dinner, sulked for a few moments; then, always the congenial sailor, joined us on deck for the rest of the day's sail.

Lovely exhibited none of the predatory behavior of most cats, but an incident one morning gave me reason to wonder if she, always the lady, had merely suppressed such impulses. Anne was in Phoenix, and I awoke alone in our forepeak bunk, to find Lovely, sitting on her haunches at the foot of the bunk, staring at me. Eyes glazed with haughty pride, her teeth were clamped tightly around the deadest, mangled sparrow I had ever seen. When I thoughtlessly admonished her and heaved the carcass overboard, Lovely tossed me a surprised, hurt glance and then slunk off into a corner of the boat to sulk for hours. She had brought me a gift, and I had failed to appreciate it.

Lovely seldom got seasick and, like a good, undemanding sailor, she was content to bunk anywhere it was convenient. Her favorite topside niche on winter days was under our inflatable, because its fabric radiated welcomed warmth from the sun. On a 500-mile round-trip cruise from San Diego out to Mexico's Guadalupe Island, she preferred a recess in one of the cockpit lockers into which she could squeeze herself to become almost invisible. Twice, unable to find her, we worried that she had gone overboard for good.

While day-sailing, one of her favorite sleeping spots was next to the boom in the curl of the mainsail's foot, where she could enjoy the sun's warmth and cooling sea breeze at the same time. We had to be alert when preparing to tack; there was the obvious danger of dumping the cat into the sea when the boom swung across. Remembering this, we merely added a mandatory "Grab the cat!" to the usual "Ready about!"

Lovely's sailing days ended when our own did. In 1986 skyrocketing costs of boating combined with work commitments forced us to sell our beloved *Gracie* and move ashore into a rented house in Coronado, California. Only during our occasional sightseeing drives along the California coast did our furry friend, face glued to the rear

*Lovely—sailor on shore leave*

window, nose sniffing the salt air, seem redeemed.

When we moved 3,300 miles cross-country to Rockport, Maine, in 1990, Lovely made it clear by her persistent but lady-like scolding that if she couldn't have a boat, at least she would like an old house which commanded a full view of Rockport Harbor. She got her wish. Both winter and summer, Lovely spent long hours at her favorite perch in a second story window, watching the daily parade of sloops, schooners, and lobstermen.

In 1993, her seventeenth year, the last of Lovely's nine lives finally gave out. Anne and I, owners of another boat by then, unsuccessfully fought back tears as we scattered her ashes, with a pinch of wildflower seeds, on a knoll amid a clump of pines only a stone's throw from Rockport Harbor, and gave a final thumbs-up salute to our friend. She was an old sailor who had, at last, come home from the sea.

≋

A former editor of *Oceans* and *Sea* magazines, Joseph E. Brown free-lances—and sails a 1955 Hinckley 36 yawl—from Rockport, Maine. New cat Whisper "entertains royally but wouldn't think of going near a boat."

# HONEYBEAR AND FAMILY

≋

### By Corrine Slade
### Norfolk, Massachusetts

I had the pleasure of residing in lovely Tenants Harbor, Maine, over an eight-year period. With me were my dogs, a family comprised of a mother, her three sons and one daughter. Each was unique in character but all were alike in their great love and devotion to one another. They had distinctive personalities that were funny, entertaining, and sometimes amazing.

Dear little Albear, a son, was light buff in color with white trim. He was usually relatively quiet and subdued, but he had a ravenous appetite. He spent time eating and then patiently waiting for his next meal or snack. Although Albear was a quiet dog, whenever he heard me packing for the trip to Maine, he would become very excited and begin jumping up and down. He would coo like a bird while he did this. With all that energy and excitement, he jumped as high as an upright person's head and never stopped until it was his turn to get into the car. Bless his mighty little heart.

Dudley-bear was also a son, black in color with white trim. He had a fascination with objects made of wood—large and long wooden objects. For instance, he would find a large log or perhaps a remnant of a 2 x 4 and pick it up in his mouth. Then, with great pride, he would prance around the perimeter of the fenced-in backyard. Afterward, he would try to enter the house with it, but of course, its span was wider than the frame of the door opening. He'd back up and move his body to the left and proceed forward. When that didn't work he'd turn his body to the right and proceed forward. Sometimes he would simply keep trying to push into the house, but whatever he did, he would not give up. He persisted as though by sheer perseverance the door would automatically widen to let him and his toy enter. The only way he

*Black Dudley and Daisy with white Ollie and Albear*

would end his struggle was on command, "Dudley, drop it!" Bless his determined little heart.

Daisy-bear was the only female out of an original litter of nine, and the boys loved and protected her all of their lives. She was the belle of the ball, the cat's meow, *la crème de la crème*, and she knew it.

What Daisy used to do was most intriguing. While her brothers barked and ran all around the yard's fencing, hoping that somehow their barking would open the gate, Daisy would be by herself in some far-off corner. What she was up to eventually became obvious. While the others were busy running and barking, she was secretly digging a hole. When the hole was large enough for an escape, she would go to the boys and direct them to it. Of course, one-by-one, they would exit. Then Daisy would quickly and enthusiastically run to the back steps, climb them to the deck and wait for a treat. I could almost swear that I saw a smile on her face at those times—possibly a testament to female superiority? Bless her cunning little heart.

Ollie-bear was a light buff-and-white-coated male, a devoted brother and son with a special attraction to seaweed. While living in Tenants Harbor, a favorite spot to take the dogs was to Marshall Point, the home of the famous Marshall Point Lighthouse. This is an amazing place, and people come here from all parts of the world, from all walks of life, young and old alike, as though to participate in the changing artistry of this land and seascape.

As soon as we would arrive, Ollie would go directly to the ocean's edge, swim out, retrieve seaweed, come back to shore, drop it, and repeat this process over and over and over again. Sometimes the seaweed was difficult to grasp, but he always persevered until he got a good mouthful of it. It seemed he was trying to collect every bit of seaweed in sight. He never tired of doing this and, needless to say, always drew a crowd.

People had different reactions. Some laughed heartily, as did I. Others simply stared in bewilderment, while still others took bets on when he would stop doing this. Well, if you had made such a bet, you would have lost. The only way Ollie would stop was to be spoken to sternly; then he knew playtime was over. Another curious thing about Ollie was that he liked to walk backward. He was a true companion and a great joy in my life. Bless his heroic little heart.

The one responsible for all of these bundles of joy, of course, was Honeybear, their mother. She was beautiful. Her black-and-white coat was wiry or "crimped." Her legs were long so that when her fur was wet it looked as though she were wearing pajamas. Everything about her was in perfect proportion—even the wonderful spirit within her.

Honeybear was the most devoted mother possible. Loyal, caring, and self-sacrificing to her puppies, she created a loving, joyous bond to them, which lasted for many years. They were a closely-knit family. They slept together each night all wrapped up among each

*Ollie—first-class retriever*

other so you couldn't tell where one began and the other ended. Even the passage of years could not erase the fact that Albear, Dudley, Daisy, and Ollie knew Honeybear was their mother. They treated her with the greatest respect, obviously different from the way they related to each other, but their bonds to each other were like nothing I had ever witnessed.

Honeybear was the love of my life— like no other dog I have ever known. She was love, joy, and everything kind and gentle in a living being. She was self suffi-cient, patient, and displayed an intelligence I have not seen before in a dog. Honeybear needed nothing to make her happy. She personified happiness twenty-four hours a

*Beautiful Honeybear*

day. If no interaction occurred, she made her own fun. If it was too cold to go for walks, she asked to be let out, barked at nothing, rolled around in the snow, snooped here and there, barked some more and then waited to be let in. This she repeated until she had expended enough energy and experienced enough exercise and fun to be satisfied for the day.

When Honeybear took food from your hand, it felt as if she were caressing your fingertips. Her greatest capacity was that of loving and enjoying life in the moment, including everything and everyone. She has provided great lessons in life for me. I am so grateful to know that my lovely Honeybear not only came into my life, but that we are bonded together, forever. Bless her kind and generous heart.

So many times I was asked by so many people what breed the dogs were. My answer was well rehearsed. "The mother came to me as a stray," I would begin. "She has been labeled everything you can imagine—from a Briard to a Kerri-Blue; from a Hungarian Puli to a combination Airdale/Shaggy Dog. I call her a mixed breed! Her pups are half of whatever she is and half Labrador."

At Marshall Point, Thomas Szelog, a highly respected wildlife photographer who lived with his wife at the lighthouse, knew the dogs well. Sometimes the couple would come out to see them. It seems that all who saw or knew the dogs were fascinated by their unique characters. Someone once referred to them as "Walt Disney Dogs" because of their especially animated personalities.

One very hot day I went to the beach for a swim in an effort to cool off. When I arrived back home the front door was slightly ajar. All the dogs were gone except Honeybear. She knew it was wrong to leave, and I have no doubt that she tried to encourage the others to remain. I searched everywhere for them but could not find them. Then a neighbor called out to me, "I seen them up tah Turkey Cove." I turned the car around and headed for that spot. To my relief and joy, there they were. All of them in the water—not swimming but bobbing, just bobbing up and down, letting the gentle swells cool them off and provide a luxurious sense of well-being. Someone else came by and said, "They'd be in theah now, nearly one-half hour."

I knew I would have a struggle getting them out, but then I remembered the car and how they loved to ride in it. I swung around and pulled up on the near side of the cove. Then I gave a toot, opened all the doors and waited. Sure enough, they came running and one-by-one climbed into the car—except for Daisy who had to be pursued. The car was an unsightly mess, but it was well worth it to have my dogs back with me and their wonder-mom Honeybear. The family was reunited and together again.

With a love and joy that challenged all others, these wonderful characters fulfilled their assigned roles in this—life's remarkable theater.

≋

Corrine Slade has a background in music, the theater, and radio. She is also a lover of dogs and cared for Honeybear and her family over a seventeen-year period. Together they found the Maine Coast and reveled in its glory, relishing the gifts it gave to them. The dogs, which were so central in her life, are gone now and, she says, a large part of herself with them. As of this writing, a new friend was keeping her busy, a year-and-a-half-old Butterscotch Wheaten Terrier named Munson.

# ITS: A MIRACLE

≈≈≈

## By Alice Boyington Farnham
### Rockland, Maine

This is a story about Its, a Seal Point Siamese cat who was named "Dacia" by our daughter Kelly when the kitten was born. When she was six weeks old she became very sick and was not expected to live. But with medicine and a lot of prayer and TLC she pulled through. After this ordeal, she was so tiny we started to call her, "Itsy Bitsy Kitty." Soon shortened to "Its," the name stuck and became official, even at the animal hospital.

When Its was born, our family lived in a mobile home park while my husband Ed was building our house. Because of all the traffic in the trailer park, we kept Its inside. Our new house was located on about 11 acres of land, most of it in fields and woods. It was also far enough from the road that we decided it was safe for her to go outside.

*Its—with Chris and Kelly Farnham when all three were very young*

Its discovered a whole new world when she started to go outdoors. There were trees to climb and tall grass to hide in. She loved to curl up and sleep in the long cool grass on hot summer days.

The many new sights and smells helped her discover the fine art of hunting.

Its loved to bring her prizes home to show us. She used a special route to return from her day's adventure, traveling out of the woods, down through the pasture, up along the back of the house, around the side, and up to the front door. In her loud, distinctive voice, Its announced all along this route that she was on her way home with something special to show us.

If Its couldn't get someone's attention right away, and her prize was too special to keep to herself, she would find the nearest open window and jump through it with her kill, hoping for praise. Her usual catches were mice, birds, moles and other small creatures, but most exciting was a live snake. She took it into Kelly's room through the open window. I was afraid of snakes and Ed wasn't home; so I called my father, who lived next door. He came over and laughed at me as he got a sock and put it on his hand. When the snake bit the end of the sock and hung on, Dad carried it outside and let it go.

Several times Its got so caught up in her hunting she didn't return home at night. She had traveled so far away and had such a long, tiring day of hunting, she decided it would be best to remain beside the brook along the lower edge of our property. In the morning, refreshed, she would start for home.

Of course, on these nights I worried about her and imagined that a larger and stronger hunter had overtaken her. But at bedtime, when our children Kelly and Christopher knelt for their prayers, we would say a special one for her. Next morning, Its would be on the doorstep asking very loudly why she had to wait to be let in for her breakfast.

When Its was four years old she disappeared for nearly a week. On Nov. 7th, I was in the kitchen cooking, and Chris and his friend were in the dining room playing. All of a sudden we heard Its coming around the house to the door, yelling painfully all the way. It had rained the night before for the first time since she'd been gone. As we later found out, she was very dehydrated. We felt that God had sent the rain to give her the strength to return home. She had been caught in a trap and, thankfully, whoever owned the trap had opened it and released her. A tine of the trap had gone completely through the knee of one back leg and also caught the tip of her tail. We immediately took her to the veterinarian, who examined her and said her leg would have to be amputated at the hip. He would also have to cut off the tip of her tail, which was by then just dead skin. "That is," the doctor said, "if you want to keep her."

"Of course I want to keep her!" I replied. So Its remained in the hospital for four days. When we picked her up, the doctor said she was still off-balance and not used to walking on only three legs; so we should keep her in a box for about a week to keep her from falling as she tried to get around.

When we got her home, we put her in a box and set it on the floor. Its jumped out and started hopping around as if she'd been that way all of her life. She climbed the stairs, jumped on chairs and beds, and used her litter box, all with no problems.

The day she came home from the hospital she was lying on her favorite chair when my father came over to visit her. Of course, she was completely shaved, and her skin was all white where the surgery had taken place. My father said her hip looked like an old cloth flour sack with the stitching at the top. Eventually the fur grew back on her hip and turned dark brown, just like the color of her other legs.

*Its—still making her rounds—fully adapted to three-legged explorations*

Its resumed her former habits and lived happily to the age of eighteen years. She was our miracle cat from the time she was born until the time of her death. Every time I let her out the door I trusted that the Lord would return her safely.

A saying I once read went through my mind each time I opened the door for her: "If you love something, set it free. If it doesn't return, it was never meant to be. If it does, love it forever."

≋

Alice Boyington Farnham is the daughter of Evelyn M. Boyington (author of *From Fear to Love* in this volume). She was born and raised in Maine and attended college at Northeast Bible Institute in Green Lane, Pennsylvania. She married a man from Vermont, and the couple lived there for two years before returning to Maine in 1976. She is the mother of two grown children and has worked as a seamstress and tailor for more than thirty years. Animals have always been a big part of her life, from cats and dogs to horses, cows, chickens, ducks, turkeys, and pigs. Now living in Rockland with her husband, 10 cats, and 11 chickens, she is at work on a book of short stories about her cats.

# WALDIE'S WORLD

~~~

### By Alice Boyington Farnham
#### Rockland, Maine

Waldie came to us in the spring of 1988. She was a sweet little Maine Coon kitten, touches of gold throughout her gray coat.

My daughter Kelly, at that time sixteen years old, brought her home from a friend's house and begged me to let her keep the kitten. Kelly had very good reasons: the kitten was the runt of the litter, and the other cats picked on her; also, very importantly, she was born on April 12th, Kelly's grandfather's birthday.

Kelly promised to take care of all the kitten's needs herself. She had a part-time job working at the veterinary hospital; so she could help buy food and pay for any vet bills. Of course I have never been able to say "no" to taking in an animal. At that time we already had two dogs, five cats and a barnyard full of ducks and chickens. In addition, Kelly and our son Chris each had a horse. So what was one more little ball of gray fur?

But I had to give my standard answer: "Ask your father." When Kelly approached him, predictably, his answer was "yes."

Kelly kept her word, and for the next two years she took very good care of Waldie. She and the cat became special friends. We had always let our cats outside, and Waldie loved the outdoors. During the day she would rather be outside than in, no matter what the weather. She would beg to be let out in pouring rain and thunderstorms—even during snowstorms, when all the other cats and dogs wanted to stay warm and dry inside. She came home by bedtime and would take herself off to Kelly's room for the night.

One night when Waldie was about two years old, she didn't come home. I called her day after day for about two weeks, but she didn't come. I prayed for her every day and finally began to give up hope.

At this time Kelly was dating Mason, the young man who lived on a farm a couple of miles from our home and would later become her husband. Kelly would often help Mason with the milking and other chores on the farm. One day she came home very excited. She said that she was positive she had seen Waldie run across the road about halfway between our house and the farm. Of course I wanted to go find her, but I knew that there were only fields, woods, and the brook, and that she would be very hard to find. But thank God she was still alive.

A few days later Kelly and Mason were at our house doing some chores when they spotted Waldie. She was very thin and very scared. She wanted to come to them but was too frightened. Finally, after talking to her and getting as close as they could, Mason reached out and grabbed her, getting scratched up in the process. When Kelly looked Waldie over, she knew something was wrong. Besides having lost weight, her front paws were swollen to almost twice the normal size.

Kelly took her to the vet and learned that her paws were swollen because skin had grown over her claws, causing her feet to become infected. Also, some of her teeth were ground down. She had been in too much pain to catch food for nourishment. The doctor removed Waldie's broken teeth, but the only thing that could be done for her feet was to declaw her. This meant that without any way to protect herself, she would have to stay inside.

Knowing that would cramp Waldie's lifestyle, I bought her a collar and took her out walking on a leash. She soon learned that she could lead people anywhere she wanted to go, and that meant away from the house. One of her reasons for the outings was to find the greenest, most luscious grass she could. She would run from one spot to the next, trying to find the best place, then sit down, eat a snack of grass and rest. This was her kind of life, and she did not want to go back inside. The only way she could be lured to leave was for her walking companion to pick a handful of her grass, pick her up and carry her back to the house. Waldie would wrap her front paws around the wrist holding the grass and eat the tasty treats all the way back to the door. Now, every time she wants to go out for a walk, she swats at the leash, which hangs on the key rack in the hallway. As soon as I put the leash on her collar, she runs to the door, bouncing up and down saying what sounds like, "out, out, out."

Soon after Waldie was declawed she had another crisis. Not realizing that she didn't have anything to hang on with, she jumped up onto a high window sill. Because she could not dig in with claws, she fell and broke her tail. The break was very close to the bottom vertebra; so the doctor had to amputate. She now wags her short stump of a tail like a little dog whenever we talk to her.

Waldie has adjusted very well to being a house cat. She gets her outings in the spring, summer and fall. Also, she has found a way to get herself soaked with her beloved water. One day after my husband Ed got out of the shower, Waldie started rubbing against his legs. Soon she realized that when anyone stepped out of the shower, the legs were wet. Rubbing against Ed's legs was not enough for her. She started a steady stream of talking, which wasn't really "meow, meow, meow," but more like "et, et, et." We took this to mean, "wet, wet, wet." Then she would bat at his feet until she made him understand that she wanted more water covering her fur. After that she would run off somewhere to groom herself.

When Ed was growing up, his family had pets, but they were not treated as part of the family as my pets were. He was raised in Vermont around farms, and each animal has a purpose and a specific job to do. Then he met me. Over our twenty-eight years of marriage he has come to realize that animals have feelings and personalities, as do humans. A lot of this he learned from Waldie. Soon after all of her problems, Ed started going through some rough times of his own. Waldie seemed to sense this. When Ed was in the house, she was always with him. When he lay down just to think and pray, she would

*Beautiful Waldie before—*

curl up close to him and purr. Waldie became very special to Ed. She helped him through a very difficult time, and he loves her for it.

It has been many years now since all of this happened. Kelly and Mason have been married for nine years. Waldie contin-ues to live with us. She is twelve years old and doesn't want anything to do with most people. I'm okay, because I feed her and take her for walks. But Ed is her special person. When she is sitting somewhere, she allows other people to pet her—only for a couple of minutes—then runs off. She is not a lap cat and will not tolerate being

*—and after asking to be wet down.*

picked up and held. But when Ed sits down in his chair in the living room, Waldie jumps onto his lap and purrs. She also sleeps curled up close to him at night. When Ed has to go away on business trips, she sleeps on his shoe or slippers or near the pillow on his side of the bed—any place she can smell his presence.

But the one thing she especially loves is her daily shower. As soon as she hears the shower curtain, Waldie bounces into the bathroom, meowing, "Wet, wet, wet, please soak me down!"

≋

Alice Boyington Farnham's stories of Its and Waldie were contributed during the very early stages of this project—in late 1999 and early 2000. Her biographical sketch is shown following the story *Its: A Miracle*.

## BRANDY—THE BLOODHOUND THAT GOT LOST

*By Sara M. Swift*
*Spencer, Massachusetts*

W e had tuned in to the local radio station and were awaiting the promised announcement that we hoped would
reunite us with our beloved Bloodhound, missing for
several days. This was a real concern, as Brandy loved his home and his
"people." Living in the midst of a heavily-populated and fairly densely-
wooded area, we were beginning to fear the worst, because it had been
rumored that a black bear had been seen in the area.

Finally the announcer's voice came through, and he seemed to be
struggling to contain laughter while he informed listeners that this was
a Bloodhound that had actually managed to get LOST. He gave the

*Brandy at home*

particulars and our location and
phone number, then apologized
for finding the whole situation
amusing, as he knew we found
no humor in it.

As a result of the radio
announcement, we received a
phone call from a woman in a
nearby town who informed us that
there had been a Bloodhound
firmly entrenched in her yard for
almost a week. It seems that her
dog Lady was in season, and
Brandy was determined not to
leave her yard. As it happened, she
lived by a lake; so Brandy had
plenty of water to drink. Also,

several of her neighbors were so worried about the canine squatter, that they had seen to it that he had the leftovers from their own meals. So, of course, Brandy was in no hurry to get home to his family.

Since Lady was to be confined for another week, it was necessary to retrieve Brandy and to bring him home to his own confinement to prevent his returning to his would-be lady-love.

So you see, Brandy's excellent Bloodhound nose didn't fail him at all, as we had thought. It had actually proved itself by discovering Lady, who lived quite a few miles away.

We had discussed having Brandy neutered but had never quite gotten around to it. Now it was a necessity. Neutering saves lives, we realized, since Brandy's route to Lady's domain had taken him through heavily traveled roads. And, of course, the fewer litters of unwanted puppies for the animal shelter to cope with, the better; especially since there are never enough adoptive homes to go around.

Brandy was neutered and, happily, stayed put after that escapade which made the family realize how much they loved him and wanted him to remain safely at home, always. He did that but also spent every one of his warm-weather weekends with his family at their summer place on the beach in Rhode Island. Although he never appeared to be much of a swimmer, he did dip a paw into the surf from time-to-time.

Unfortunately Brandy didn't have a long life. Cancer took him when he was just six years old.

〰

Sara Swift lives in the woods and has 50 acres for her animals to run through—also in which to observe all kinds of wildlife, including deer and an occasional wandering black bear. Always an animal- and bird-lover, she has never been without pets, including squirrels, baby raccoons, possums, turtles, baby orphaned birds, goats, pet hens, a young calf, a donkey, ducks, and many cats and dogs. Twice widowed, she has three children, twelve grandchildren, and three great-grandchildren. A "self-proclaimed artist," her favorite subjects for oil paintings are animals. As of this writing she has one dog, a thirteen-year-old German Shorthair Pointer.

*The following story appeared in the " Moorings Moments" section of*
Sail *magazine, Vol. 31, No. 3, March 2000. It is reproduced here, courtesy
of* Sail, *with permission of the author. The author also kindly provided
photographs (not included in the original article) to illustrate this incident in
the British Virgin Islands (BVI).*

## DOG TRAINS MAN IN BVI

### By Loron Holden
#### Foley, Alabama

Upon awakening from a dreamy night of sleeping in the cockpit of our charter, I suddenly had the feeling that I was not
alone! Even though my crew had crept into their cabins
shortly after watching another brilliant sunset in the BVI, I had company. A quick but careful investigation revealed a large ball of black fur
curled up at my feet. Soon I was looking eye to eye with one very large
black island dog. Since we were anchored several yards off-shore this
was quite a shock!

I called softly to
my first mate. Since
neither of us is very
brave when it comes
to large animals, we
quietly decided that
the best way to clear
the decks was to
entice this animal
from the unknown
into the dinghy. So a
quick breakfast was
prepared for our
stowaway and placed

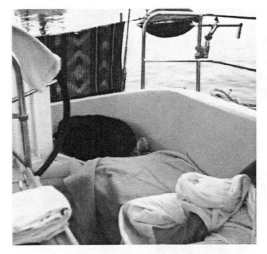

*A large ball of black fur was curled up at my feet*

in the dinghy. Without any hesitation, the dog jumped into the dinghy and quickly devoured our offering. After the meal he simply sat down in the bow of the dinghy and looked longingly toward shore.

*Ferrying our guest toward shore*

Since I had now decided that he was not vicious and was not hungry, I boarded the dinghy, started the engine and headed for the beach. Once we touched sand the dog jumped from the dinghy. I did a quick reverse, turned the dinghy and headed for our boat.

About halfway back I noticed my crew waving in my direction and pointing toward the beach. There was our furry breakfast guest swimming toward another anchored boat! He promptly swam to the stern of the boat, climbed the stern ladder with ease and assumed the position for breakfast number two! I had just been trained, island

*Going for breakfast number two* style!

≋

Loron Holdon is a native of Washington, having attended high school in Richland and obtained a bachelor's degree from the University of Texas. During his years in the electrical industry, he and his family were able to live in many different locations throughout the United States. He is now building a new retirement home in Foley, Alabama.

Loron describes his family as being "avid water people who enjoy all kinds of water sports, especially our charter experiences in the BVI," one of which resulted in the meeting with the black island dog. His account of that meeting in *Sail* magazine won the prize of a seven-day charter on a 50-foot sail boat for him and his family, including his wife, a son and daughter-in-law, a daughter and son-in-law, and, for his first real sailing adventure, a five-year-old grandson. A second trip to the same location brought no further news of the resourceful canine visitor to their vessel.

# BESA'S RESCUE

≋

## By Alison Riefe-Turnbull
### Rockport, Maine

It was May, and the temperature of the waters of Penobscot Bay edged toward a brisk 50 degrees, just about right for a dip by a Labrador Retriever. After all, Labs had been trained to help fishermen pull heavy surf nets in the frigid waters of the North Atlantic.

One Saturday afternoon I borrowed my brother's dog, Besa (pronounced Bee´sa), a year-old black Lab, and we headed toward a remote spot on Beauchamp Point in Rockport. Just as I anticipated, she took to the water like an otter, fetching sticks, the Frisbee, and a tennis ball. As she was swimming out to retrieve the Frisbee, she caught sight of a big, brightly-painted lobster buoy bobbing in the surf several yards away. I instantly realized this could be a problem if she decided to swim out and try to bring back the buoy for the next round of fetch. Indeed, that was her intention, and she swam off to get the buoy despite my commands to return to me.

I yelled at Besa at the top of my lungs—to no avail. Becoming increasingly concerned, I looked around for signs of other people in the area or passing boats that could help me distract her from her quest of bringing back the lobster buoy anchored to the bottom of the Bay. No such luck. She was wrestling with the buoy with such determination I realized that she was not coming back without it. Not knowing what else to do, I ran to my car, dialed 911, and reached the dispatcher at the Rockport Police Station. After hearing my frantic report, she said she would send an officer to see if he could help.

Soon an officer arrived, and he, too, stood on the edge of the rocks calling to Besa, with no results. By now she had been in the water a considerable amount of time, and we both realized she was becoming sluggish in her struggle. At this point the officer began to remove his

*Besa hunting—ready to pounce*

shoes and belt, and I thought he was going to go in to get her. We both continued to call to her, throwing in sticks and such to try to divert her attention and get her to come back to shore.

Besa was beginning to founder—floundering about trying to keep her head up while still hanging onto the buoy—when the policeman finally said to me, "I don't think she's going to last much longer." With fear and terror in my heart at the thought of losing this beautiful, faithful dog to the depths of the sea, I plunged in and swam what seemed a very long distance in the numbing water. I grabbed her by her collar and as I began to pull her away from the buoy, she gave up her quest. I turned her around in the direction of the rocks and gave her a push while the officer called her name over and over. We reached the rocky water's edge, and the policeman grabbed Besa by the collar and lifted her exhausted body from the water while I struggled to pull myself up onto the rocks and regain my breath. As a weary Besa and I shivered on the rocks, the policeman congratulated me and stroked Besa, who mustered enough energy to wag her tail in appreciation.

A point of interest, after the fact, is that just before I plunged in, the officer told me that, legally, he could not jump into the Bay to rescue Besa. In retrospect, I am thankful that his fateful words snapped me into doing what I knew I had to do. I am just glad that he was there to watch and make sure that we both arrived back safely. After a few minutes in the car with the heat on full blast I felt better as, I presume, did Besa. Sometime later, as I relived this episode in memory, I understood how a 90-pound woman could push a Steinway grand piano out of a burning building!

≋

The author submitted no biographical information, preferring to focus on Besa's story.

## SHADOW'S SURPRISE

≋

### By Harvey Versteeg
Augusta, Maine

Many years ago, my wife and I were canoeing on the Huron River in Michigan. In the middle of the canoe was our then-young black Poodle, Shadow. Around one bend, we passed a canoe going in the opposite direction with another dog in the middle. Shadow perked up and looked, then decided to go visit the other dog. Never having had swimming lessons, he seemed to think he could just walk over to visit his new friend.

He jumped out of the canoe and immediately sank. Rising quickly to the surface, paddling for his life, he had the most surprised look on his face, as if to say, "What went wrong?" We pulled him back aboard where he shook the water off, reinforcing the old saying, "Nobody loves a wet dog."

But we did love him for all the time we had him. He liked to eat veggies. He would clean up the scrapings after someone peeled carrots or apples, and when given the opportunity, he would eat salad. Shadow was a treasure who left a large empty place in our lives when he died twenty-five years ago at age fifteen.

≋

As a teen, Harvey Versteeg hitchhiked 17,000 miles around the country—from Michigan to Idaho via New Orleans and El Paso, then back to Michigan through Fairbanks, Alaska, and across Canada. He has parachuted 13 times (in Idaho and Montana) fighting fires as a U.S. Forestry Service smoke jumper and 11 times as a lieutenant with the 101st Airborne Division.

A 1956 graduate of Michigan State University, Harvey has taught school in Alaska, Michigan, and Maine, run history museums for fifteen years in three states, designed the logo for the submarine USS

*Augusta*, and helped design buildings and military training simulators. He is retired from work in highway design at the Maine Department of Transportation.

Harvey met his wife in Michigan, where she did medical research after graduating from the University of Maine-Orono. When their family was established, she earned a degree in computer technology and business and now works as a senior program analyst for the State of Maine. Their son is a computer software trouble-shooter in Boston, and their daughter is a special education teacher, sign language interpreter, and church youth leader in Maine.

Harvey and his wife have deep roots in the Northeast. His family settled in Pennsylvania in 1680; hers has been in Maine since 1635. The Versteegs presently live in the old Augusta farmhouse where she grew up.

Harvey says two factors produced Shadow's name: a) he was black and b) he followed his master around like a shadow. He continued this behavior with the Versteegs' young daughter—now grown "but still attracting pets and people wherever she goes."

## André and Sprocket: A Perfect Match

≋

### By Sarah Rheault
#### Camden, Maine

My late husband, André, grew up in Boston surrounded by dogs and a donkey. Through most of his life he had at least two canine companions, but the one that meant the most to him in all of his seventy-two years was Sprocket, who, sadly, died just a few short months after André did.

The first dogs in Andy's life—all while he was still at home—were a Sealyham Terrier named Toto, a Great Dane/Newfoundland mix named Charbon, a Shepherd named Cazon, and a Labrador named Michael.

As an adult Andy had, through the years, a Dachshund/Beagle mix called Piper, and a series of Long-haired Dachshunds. Before we were married these were Peppo, Topsy, and Saf Saf; also a Cardigan Corgi named Fango, who was born in the Solomon Islands. After our marriage we adopted a Solomon Islands Special (bush dog) called Meta.

Nearly all of these dogs had names linked to significant elements or geographic locations in Andy's life or our life together. For example, Saf Saf was named for a café in Tunisia; Meta for the Metanico River in the Solomon Islands.

At the time of our marriage, I gave Andy a Long-haired Dachshund named Moffatt. He came from England to the islands to join Meta and was named after a good (British) friend, Hamish Moffatt. We also acquired from the Islands a cat called Mao. Later, after we moved to Maine with Moffatt and Mao, we acquired another Long-haired Dachshund, Pinga, named after an island in the Pacific. Pinga became Moffatt's first wife. His second wife, Samba von Rockport, of the same breed, came from New England. Eventually, about a year after all had departed, we found Sprocket, who was by far the most loved of all of Andy's pets.

Sprocket, notwithstanding the masculine-sounding name, was a beautiful female. Her mother was, questionably, a Setter/Labrador mix; her father a well-known, purebred Portuguese Water Dog in Camden, Maine. Sprocket's mother and her large litter of puppies had been abandoned. No single shelter could handle them all, so the little ones had to be separated. Several puppies together were taken to other shelters, but the mother and two of her puppies were taken to the Camden-Rockport shelter. This is where we adopted Sprocket ten years ago when she was four months old.

*Quiet vigil in a 1959 Morris Minor 1000—
awaiting Andy's return*

We had help from our children and a friend in selecting a name for our lively puppy. The name came from a children's television show, *Fraggle Rock*, where two people wore a dog suit. When our puppy was little, she seemed loose in her skin, and one of our friends commented that she looked like a person in a dog suit. The television two-person dog was named "Sprocket;" so our children decided on that for her name.

In spite of her mixed heritage, Sprocket's Water Dog ancestry was dominant. Portuguese Water Dogs are known to be water creatures *par excellence*. Historically, they were used by European fishermen to round up schools of fish, to bring broken nets back to the boat, and even, it is said, to carry messages from boats to the shore. Sprocket had a similar love of and familiarity with the water—in a puddle, at a lake, or at the edge of the sea.

From the beginning, her associations with humans and the ocean were superb. Her predecessor, Moffatt, one of the many Long-haired Dachshunds, was also a water lover, but he had a law—Moffatt's law— that governed his actions in a body of water, be it a puddle or the ocean. He would always go in just minutes before it was time to come home or get into the car. Sprocket, on the other hand, during warmer weather, would spend every moment she could in the water—wading, sitting, or standing. And, if the truth be known, going to the bathroom in the seaweed was a must for her.

When she wasn't wading in the water somewhere or lying in the seaweed, rubbing her nose in it, sometimes eating it, she would sit on the dock watching ducks, gulls, and other sea birds. She was amused by the water and very funny at times while playing with the waves on the beach at Cape Cod. But mostly she liked to sit or lie in the water at the shore.

Sprocket wasn't a swimmer the way Labs are. But year-'round, whether in a puddle, a stream, or sloshing around in the sea-weed at low tide, she would immerse herself just to get wet, no matter what the temperature. Then she would come out, shake herself (considerately, away from people), and be refreshed. Occasionally, during the winter months,

*Sprocket sloshing around in the seaweed at low tide*

she would sit in an icy puddle and come out with icicles hanging from her long, curly coat!

Portuguese Water Dogs are said to be "mouthy," wanting to chew or hold objects in their mouths. As a puppy this was certainly true of Sprocket. She chewed on everything she could get into her mouth. Later, as an adult, she wanted to hold us close in a variety of ways. When we were standing, she would lean against a leg to let us know she was there. But if that leg were moved, she would continue to lean toward it until she almost toppled over. Or, if we were sitting down, she would support a hand with her paw and move it to her chest to be scratched.

*En route during an outing with Andy and the author
in a 1929 Model A Ford Phaeton.*

Sprocket was Andy's perfect companion. They often went sailing together, which was a joy. But she made it a little difficult while riding in the rowboat or canoeing. She liked to go from side to side, which made steering something of a challenge. And walking along the beach together gave ample opportunity for shared quiet moments or spirited play.

*Sharing moments of joy
Ballston Beach, Cape Cod*

Then, of course, there was that wonderful closeness when riding together in a car. Andy had a major passion for old cars, and Sprocket loved to ride with him, especially in a convertible with the top down. On such occasions, when either of us separately or both of us together parked in town, Sprocket would sit silently, confident and self-contained in the open vehicle until either or both of us returned.

Intermittently, she would stand to give a warm greeting to anyone who stopped to pat her; then she would sit again and continue her quiet vigil.

Aside from special outings with either of us alone, Sprocket came with us everywhere and showed equal devotion to both of her human companions. When next to the driver of the car, for example, she was most content when she could place her paw on the driver's hand when it rested on the seat or on the gearshift. She was a warm, loving part of everything we did.

When we went swimming, she would stay on the beach, keeping an eye on us and everything around. When we would lie on the sand for sunbathing, she would be beside us. And whenever we sat on the deck at our camp in Cushing, Maine, she would sit between us. If we were together in a room, she divided her time between us—periodically moving close to one and then the other. She was very much a family-oriented companion, totally devoted and loyal to both of us.

Sprocket had so many virtues it is not surprising that she was the most loved of all of my husband's pets. They were a perfect match for each other and for me. I hope this memoir of good times and a wonderful relationship will bring joy to others also.

≋

Sarah Rheault was born in England but grew up in central Africa in what is now Zambia. Later, while living in Ghana and Nigeria, she and her younger sister were sent to boarding school and college in England. Sarah's training in hotel management led her to Australia, where she managed a ski lodge, and to the Solomon Islands, where she met her husband, André.

Pets have always been important in Sarah's life, and she recalls the antics of one of the British Bulldogs in the family when they lived in Zambia. Her name was "Sally," and she loved both cats and babies. She would swirl the family cat around in the air by its tail until the cat had had enough and would dig its claws into the dog's nose to ensure a quick release. Also, whenever Sally saw any of the local nannies pushing a baby by in a pram, she would rush out, grin at the baby, and, in the process, manage to scare the nanny up a tree, so to speak.

After she was married, Sarah recalls with special delight the weekends in the British Solomon Islands when she and André would go with their dogs Meta and Moffatt to a nearby river. Donning masks, they would float down to the sea, with the dogs swimming and frolicking beside them—a wonderful way to stay cool so close to the equator.

During their years together Sarah and André raised one daughter and one son. They were entrepreneurs in various types of businesses linked to the sea, including ocean-related commerce in Guadalcanal and boat building in Rockport. Following their move to Midcoast Maine they were both active in community affairs and served on diverse boards of directors according to their respective talents and interests. Sarah continues in several such capacities as of this writing. And, recently, she adopted a Great Dane mix named Kennebec.

# DUCK RESUSCITATION

≈

## By Sam Jones
### Lincolnville, Maine

They weren't really pets, but I had fed them every morning during the winter months for more than twenty years. They were ducks that became "my" ducks, because I formed an attachment to them. Anywhere from 20 to 75 would collect on the Megunticook River near the back door of the drugstore on Main Street in Camden that I owned—the Boynton-McKay Drug Store, established in 1893.

One late winter morning several years ago, I went out the back door of the drug store to feed the resident ducks their cracked corn. As I scattered the corn on the ice in the river, a flock of perhaps 20 ducks arrived and began scooping up the corn. Their appetites were terrific. I watched them for a few minutes and noticed the ice beginning to crack under their weight. They continued to gorge themselves, seeming not to mind that the corn began floating on the frigid water. I went back inside to begin my day of pharmacy. A few minutes later, when I glanced out the window to see if anything was left, all the ducks but one were gone, and that one was in trouble.

When the ice cracked, the corn began sliding off into the water between two sheets of ice. This last hungry duck had thrust his head under the sheet next to the one he was standing on to grab a few kernels. When the sections of ice came back together he was stuck with his head under water. Now his wings were moving feebly as he struggled to free his head. He was drowning.

I raced out the door, over the railing of the deck, and onto the riverbank. Gritting my teeth, I waded into the icy water up to my knees. By that time all wing movement had stopped. I pushed one sheet of ice down to free the duck's head and picked up the limp body.

As I climbed back up to the deck, I let the head hang down to release as much water as possible. I massaged his chest and throat as I hurried back into the store, yelling for someone to call my wife Ronda. I took the duck to the warmest place in the store, the furnace room, and continued to rub his chest. After a short time he started to cough, and a lot of water ran out of his mouth. Things were looking up.

Ronda arrived a few minutes later, and we headed for the Camden Hospital for Animals with the sputtering patient, who was beginning to struggle. There they put him into an oxygen cage, and we hoped for the best as we headed back to Boynton-McKay. Within an hour we got a call from the hospital and were told that he was ready to go back into the river.

We provided the transportation, but this time, to our surprise, the recovered duck settled down nicely in my arms. He was breathing well and let me hold him with no trace of a struggle. He felt very much like a real pet. Once back at the river, I relaxed my hold and let this very lucky duck go. He flew down to the water and just swam away. In his own way he had thanked us for our concern. Although he had no special markings that would let us identify him thereafter, we are sure he returned as long as he could to a special spot on the river where he knew there were friends.

≋

The author submitted no biographical information, preferring to focus on the duck's story.

# MUTINY ON A TIN BOAT OR CATO'S FIRST SWIM

≋

### By Al Holzman
#### S.V. Strait Aero, Waikiki, Hawaii

It was raining crabs and dogs. "Crabs and dogs" was a little joke between Cato and me. You see, in addition to being First Mate of the Sailing Vessel *Strait Aero*, Cato was also Ship's Cat.

Cato T. Cat was a true sea cat. He was born aboard *K.M.*, a New Zealand-built Polynesian catamaran. That's where he was when my children and I met up with him in Pokai Bay, Oahu.

From where we lay at anchor the sound of kittens was audible across the water. Our crew list had an opening for Ship's Cat; so we paid a visit to the little catamaran.

*K.M.*'s captain was inclined to let as many of the kittens ship out as we would care to sign on. Cato seemed eager to expand his horizons. His pedigree was impeccable. His mother had joined *K.M.* at Tahiti, and his father (apparently) was an "aristocat" of the Ala Wai Boat Yard.

Cato didn't know that we were bound for Alaska, but true to his calling (after a short bout of *mal-de-mer*) he sailored on. A month later we made our landfall at Sitka, and continued on to the tiny fishing village of Yakutat. (To stay afloat I had located the bane of a sailor's existence—a shore job).

It was on Yakutat's somewhat shaky ground that Cato first learned about *terra firma*—and shrews and flickers and swallows and bears. He didn't care much for bears but found the lesser creatures to his liking (excepting the swallows which harassed him mercilessly).

A fringe benefit of the job was the use of an old tin rowboat. We used it to raid some of our clients' crab-pots (I had, more or less, secured the owners' permissions as long as I re-baited them).

So, that's what we were about when it commenced to rain as it hadn't since Noah became a sailor. We had set out in the usual coastal

*Cato at his fairweather post as look-out on the bow—Yakutat Bay, Alaska*

Alaskan drizzle that is 90 percent mist and 10 percent rain. However, by the time we had pulled the third, and farthest-from-the-dock, crab-pot, the ratio had reversed.

There was a nice supper's worth of Dungeness crabs scuttling about in the rainwater that had collected in the bottom of the boat as I pulled for home. There is nothing quite like a good stiff row to windward. Ah … the invigorating salt air with the smell of decaying mud flats combined with cold rain seeping through the seams and fly of one's foul weather gear … these are pleasures denied the Immortals but generously bestowed upon the common waterman.

Cato was speaking to these pleasures (I'm sure) from under the midships seat, when one of the crabs decided to invade his space. Using his better judgment, Cato fled to his usual (fair weather) post as lookout on the bow. It was from there that he espied a small, uninhabited, though densely vegetated, island. Something snapped in that loyal heart, and the iron discipline of the sea melted. Without a trace of hesitation, he went over the side.

He surfaced with hair slicked back, ears laid flat against his little skull, cat-paddling like crazy for that cozy looking, non-tropical, jungle island.

It's a sad thing when generations of tradition are broken by the impetuous act of a young sailor. Sailors are born and bred to endure hardships and abuse with a smile on their faces and gratitude in their hearts. I couldn't allow Cato to make this grievous error. How would he ever face himself in the morning? The bully cats, squabbling over fish entrails at the cold storage plant, would jeer at him.

"Avast there! Ye'll not get away with that, you Lubber!" I vowed as I slewed the boat around and laid on the oars to cut him off.

Cato veered neither port nor starboard, steering straight for that humanly-impenetrable jungle island of Salmon Berry brambles and Devil's Club—that cold and soggy varmint haven. It was a near thing. Running aground in the muck, I rescued him from that shameful fate by the narrowest of margins. Springing to the bow, I grabbed him by the neck and slung him back on board. Looking like a malnourished water rat, he meekly burrowed under my rain jacket to snuggle against my warm belly (Arrgh!) for the rest of the trip back to the dock.

We survived Alaska, and Cato lived to enjoy many more hardships of the sea, such as dining on flying fish under the Southern Cross and seeking out his relatives along the waterfronts of various Pacific ports. But never again did I see him take another swim—voluntarily.

The author submitted no biographical information, preferring to focus on Cato's story.

# REGGIE—THE CRUISING CORGI

By *Ann Sziklas*
*Camden, Maine*

**B**orn in the Midwest and transported to New England at the age of eight weeks, Reggie came into our lives after we began spending summers on a sailboat. He happily joined us aboard rather than be left behind. It soon became evident that he had the same tolerance level as his mistress, also a Midwesterner, and they would complain in unison to the skipper whenever conditions at sea became unpleasant. But he learned the meaning of "hard-a-lee," and when the crew was busy handling the boat, he would wedge himself against a leeward bulkhead and quietly endure.

*Reggie—the perfect cruising companion with the author's grandson Will*

In general Reggie's major chore aboard was to keep the floor under the dining table cleared of crumbs. In his later years he welcomed grandchildren aboard (more crumbs). But what he enjoyed most was going ashore in the dinghy to stretch his short legs and explore the islands. He sailed with us along the shores of southern New England before we moved permanently to the better cruising grounds of the Maine coast.

A favorite beach was on Butter Island in East Penobscot Bay, where he and his mistress would hunt for a special lucky stone, a smooth, dark stone with a white ring around it. Some beaches are deceiving, though. During

*Umm—interesting scents in the morning breeze*

one visit to Winter Harbor on Vinalhaven Island, Reggie sank deep into black Maine mud, dooming himself to a thorough dunking before he could return to the big boat. Other favorites were Frenchboro and the Cranberry Islands, with their pleasant trails and friendly residents.

Many of the harbors along the Maine coast are excellent for sailing small boats. After dropping anchor, one can explore all the nooks and crannies in a sailing dinghy. Reggie often accompanied his mistress on these excursions, choosing to suffer a wet bottom rather than worry about her safe return. Just before sunset, when the wind had abated, evening sails in Burnt Coat Harbor on Swan's Island or in Blue Hill were happy times for them. He even went along as crew in the "Goin' to the Dogs Regatta"— races for sailboats under 20 feet, sponsored by *Maine Boats & Harbors* magazine

*Flaked out on the foredeck*

to benefit the Camden-Rockport Animal Rescue League. No matter that they did not win; they enjoyed sailing together in the dinghy.

Our wonderful Corgi was the perfect cruising companion—devoted, patient, ever cheerful whatever the weather or conditions at sea.

We miss him.

≋

The author submitted no biographical information, preferring to focus on Reggie's story.

*Reggie and the author enjoying a sail together in the dinghy*

# THE SHEENA STORIES

≈

## By Hannah Merker
## Bristol, Maine

*We wish to acknowledge that the stories contributed by Hannah Merker to this volume have appeared in different forms in the following publications:*

The *Sheena—Professional Hearing Dog* story, in various forms, has appeared in:

*Time Being Made of Moments*, by Hannah Merker, 1985

*Listening; Ways of Hearing in a Silent World*, by Hannah Merker; first edition, 1994; second edition, 2000; four foreign editions

*Hearing Loss*, bimonthly Journal of SHHH (Self Help for Hard of Hearing People)

*Seniority*, 1984 (a magazine now out of production)

*North Shore Woman's Newspaper*, 1985 (Long Island, N.Y.)

*Northeast*, 1984 (Sunday Magazine of the *Hartford Courant*)

*My Weekly*, 1984 (England and Ireland)

The *Sheena's Legacy* story and *Elegy for Sheena* have appeared in:

*Hearing Health*, 1995 (a national publication)

*Academic Library Book Review* (Elegy only), 1994, October issue.

All three Sheena contributions are included here with permission of the author.

## SHEENA—PROFESSIONAL HEARING DOG
## PART I

≋

### By Hannah Merker
### Bristol, Maine

When was it—when did I first realize that my large brindle Boxer was telling me there was a knock at our door, when the telephone rang, when an erratic sound was present around me? As we walked at dawn, at dusk, I was pushed to one side if a car surged behind us; I was awakened as the sun rose by a lick on my face. When did the radio and the alarm clock cease to register to my senses as heard?

My dog was old, quite ill, yet I clung to this creature that most understood my muffled world. What would I do without him? Attached to me since a pup, Barney had become my ears, interpreting sounds around me, conveying to me life messages one sense did not receive.

It is not unusual for animals to attach themselves to a person, responding to that person's specific needs. An amazing connection can take place over the years.

I was living on the Good Ship *Bette Anne*, an ancient houseboat, with Barney and a constantly changing population of cats. Unknown to me, a friend called the Guide Dog Foundation for the Blind in Smithtown, New York, not far from where I lived. They had recently been given an anonymous gift to train several dogs for the deaf and hearing impaired. Their trainers came to see me, watching my ways of handling my seriously ill dog. They needed to know me and my environment in order to choose the most suitable dog for me. They could see that Barney had become a life-support system for me.

Sheena had already completed training in basic obedience skills. She was skilled, too, in responding to specific sounds and knew how to report them. The ring of a telephone, a tap on a door, a baby crying, would bring her to her owner indicating she had a message to convey. Soon I would see her transfer her allegiance from her trainer to me. But at the beginning, while Barney still lived, only the trainers came to my home. I knew nothing about my future companion. I did not ask.

Sheena was brought to the swaying docks and waterfront life of Port Jefferson, a harbor community not far from my own. She was being prepared to adapt to my specific needs and the unusual things she would need to know living on a boat.

Barney died in June 1982. A week before, he lost his own hearing. For that week, and the days after, until Sheena came to me, I had time to absorb the shocking impact of isolation when certain kinds of communication are cut off. I did not know when a visitor was at my door. I was unaware of a leak, one evening, flooding a room not ten feet from me.

Sheena, a year-and-a-half-old orange fluff of energy with doe-like eyes, arrived with her trainers, gentle intuitive people. Curious, alert, she impishly tested my orders, which might be a voice command, a hand signal, a certain tug on her leash. We worked together, learning to live together, with the trainers visiting and helping us often. The edge of efficiency was on her side. She knew what to do. Her training was exceptional. Still, life on the water was a huge Pandora's chest.

*The author with Sheena*

A licensed hearing guide dog, Sheena was found in a kennel. She had been either lost or abandoned at a tender age. Whenever asked what breed she was I would reply, "One-hundred-percent everything." On her collar I etched her qualifications: PHD—(Professional Hearing Dog).

A hearing guide dog's expertise is in the field of sound—the quality and meaning of sound—from the softest whispers to the deepest of thundering roars. Sheena knew she must constantly assess everything, consider its meaning, and creatively be able to transmit the meaning of the sound, the significance of the sound's occurrence, and the fact that the sound is present.

Sheena's ever-ongoing training involved participating in long, arduous studies in various aspects of language—verbal, vernacular, vulgar, and voluptuous (body language). Basically, within the field of communications, a hearing guide dog is a translator, a specialized and demanding vocation.

On any ordinary day, Sheena would lie on the dock beside our floating home, the Good Ship *Bette Anne*, moored at a slip in a marina on Glen Cove Creek on the north shore of Long Island, New York. A clear caressing easterly wind might ruffle her orange locks. Large white puffs of clouds would hang high overhead under a dark blue late August sky. Leaves on the shore-side trees in the wildlife preserve across the narrow creek would already show deep reds and browns. Tall eelgrass at the edge of the tide is yellow, its crisp green gone since late July. The eelgrass swishes with an almost imperceptible sigh. Soon, late September, early October, it will turn to straw, crackling in the wind. Sheena would find ways to tell this to me, her special human companion.

Lying on the dock, Sheena was always working. Several people walked by. Some leaned over to greet her. She extended a paw. She knew who was coming long before footsteps reached her. Heavy steps, light steps, eager or hesitant steps told her who was there.

Strangers tested all of her skills. In the beginning Sheena informed me of the presence of anyone coming down the boatyard ramp to the dock. After a while she would come to me at the typewriter with bristling excitement for friends, or with ears pointed up, her paw insistent on my knee, for unknowns.

In such cases, rushing back to our deck, she would start barking, a fierce fiery forecast of threat for a stranger, a chorus of welcome for a friend, her wagging or drooping tail, the position of her ears, telling me what her barking alone could not. I could not, after all, hear her bark. Long before a person would reach us, I would know what Sheena was telling me: "This is a friend." "That is an unknown, but probably we can trust him." Occasionally, she would announce, "THIS IS AN ENEMY." With her innate ability to judge human nature, she always sensed when someone was anti-canine.

Sheena's alertness continued even when she was inside, even when sleeping across my toes, even when she was dog-tired. This was part of the commitment she made when she was finally accepted into the exclusive professional society of hearing ear dogdom. Hearing guide dogs seem to promise that neither rain nor snow, cold nor heat, or gloom of night in an electrical failure or lack of a fresh bone or temptation to run and romp with other boatyard four-footed friends, will stay them from the continuing completion of appointed tasks. The rewards were sufficient. Sheena loved being someone's ears.

An ordinary day with Sheena began as light appeared on the eastern horizon. I do not have an alarm clock, although Sheena was trained to respond to one. We would go through our awakening routine easily without one. I happen to love mornings. When Sheena, asleep on her settee beside me, sensed the coming dawn, when she heard the early songs of shore birds, she would stretch and wait. When there seemed to be more light than dark, when she noticed egrets and night herons feeding close by in the peopleless peace of the early hour on the creek, Sheena would lean over and begin to lick my face. If I sank back on the pillow, she would lean over to me again. She was a superior alarm clock. She would not go away. She could not be ignored or turned off until I would respond. Eventually, I was happy with her persistence. I do relish the early morning hours.

Once I agreed to face the day and began stretching, Sheena quickly did some reconnaissance work, checking to see where Sarah had left her evening catch. Sarah, a five-year-old feline, worked nights. She patrolled the dock and the yard, bringing home dead rats, dead fish, and other dead creatures. Most of the time her gifts were left on deck. Sheena would alert me to the nuisance, knowing I suffered so if I accidentally stepped on something odd before I was fully awake.

During the day, Sheena listened for the telephone. She listened to the hissing of our many creek swans. She listened for helicopters flying low overhead. She listened for the water pump, which I always forgot to turn off and makes an awful sound. She listened for fish jumping, geese honking, to the flapping wings in August when some of our wildlife prepared to leave us.

She listened to the wind, noting its changing direction, perhaps its rising force. She even listened for thunder, which terrified her. And for each, she had a signal, a way of translating the happening of the sound into my quiet world. I still could not hear these things after Sheena told me, but now I knew they were there, recalling that once I knew without conscious thought that sound is connected to the swaying willow, the gull. Now I glance at the swaying eelgrass and perhaps see the wind, know its force and energy by how much the eelgrass is leaning, perhaps remember the soft sigh of its swish in the spring, the crisp crackle when it yellows in the fall.

Most of the time Sheena would just come to me, turning to the source of sound, her calm or agitation expressing the magnitude of the sound, of the noise, of the moment.

I travel with my guide dogs a little each day on ordinary errands or to the library for research. Sheena's favorite times were when we went to class, where I taught English courses and creative writing. At the front door of the building I would drop her leash, watching her race up the stairs to the classroom where everyone would greet her. She loved being center-stage. After a while she would climb onto my desk and listen. She audited all of my classes—hoping, I imagine, to develop her writing skills.

Sometimes we went out to restaurants. If it were a place we had not visited before, Sheena knew what to expect. We would be greeted with "No pets allowed here." Another person would come forth, some important official, trying to usher us out. I am always quite firm now, much better than I used to be. It is important for people to know about hearing dogs and their rights. They are permitted to be with their special persons in public places. Sheena knew what her mission was and what was expected of her. Standing beside me during such con-frontations, in dignity, her fur brushed to shining auburn highlights, she would wait at my left heel. We are both immovable objects.

With a small smile, I present our legal identification, along with our civil rights in the particular state in which we reside. These declare my dog's legal status. In such situations we are invariably led to a dis-tant table, a secluded corner away from other diners, with the *maitre d'* casting apologies hither and yon as we pass by. We do not mind. We love to be away from the crowd. Sheena would crawl to her expected place over my left shoe, eagerly licking up crumbs under the table. She was never thanked for this service.

On the other hand, we often dined at our favorite Chinese restau-rant where Sheena was lovingly greeted by Paul, the owner. We had our regular table by a partition and a tranquil pond. Paul presents me with my martini, just the way I like it, before I even ask. Then he asks permission to go downstairs—meaning under the table, to talk to Sheena. He slips her two or three fortune cookies even though he has been told not to feed her. Paul makes a big fuss over her presence. Fortune cookies were Sheena's favorite food.

And so it is evening, the wind rising. Perhaps a storm follows.

*One of Sheena's boatyard cat companions—*
*Elijah aboard the sloop* Haimish

Sheena checks the boat for leaking water. Nothing today. But we have an interesting visitor. Sheena rushes to me, grabbing my skirt, bringing me over to a small table. A ladybug! I am elated. Ladybugs mean good luck. Thank goodness Sheena did not eat it. I think she was about to. It may have appeared to be more tasty than her usual fresh meat snacks of flies and bees. O well, she knows she will be getting a bone tonight. A barbecue is warming up down the dock. A neighboring fisherman always grilled steak, giving Sheena the bone.

Now it is dark. A flock of geese soars overhead; so lovely. Are they from Canada or leaving us? We have some resident geese that do not migrate. Or are they just off for an evening jaunt? Sheena liked the geese. They did not hiss at her like the swans. And she tells me that Jay, another liveaboard, is practicing his trombone. I did not know he had one until Sheena led me down to his boat one night. I thanked her, saying that sometimes there are blessings to being deaf.

If this night is an ordinary night, we might have a visit from raccoon. He swims over from land, visiting us first. I tell Sheena to keep a distance from him, that he could tear her to pieces. She, of course, felt she could defend herself. Besides, her barks would awaken the whole dock. Her orange tresses rose in anger (maybe fear?) when raccoon climbed on deck.

I have barely mentioned how Sheena was trained for a water life, about traveling in airplanes, and about our veterinarian who makes houseboat calls. I have not mentioned that her photos have been sold to help finance the cat food, the dog food, cheese snacks and bones, and radishes. Oh, how Sheena loved radishes. And now, with her open, inquiring mind, she has a new passion—an almost irresistible urge: to taste a ladybug.

Sheena was proud of her credentials:

PHD (Professional Hearing Dog);

LNYGD (Legal New York Guide Dog);

HES (Hearing Ear Specialist);

MS (Master of Sound);

DL (Doctor of Listening);

TLS (Translations with Love and Sensitivity).

And for over twelve years—a loving and beloved companion: my ears.

*Sheena in her favorite spot, the bowsprit of the sloop* Haimish

## SHEENA'S LEGACY
## PART II

≈

### By Hannah Merker
Bristol, Maine

She did not request early retirement—commonplace among guide dogs beyond octogenarian years in the canine calibration of age. Belying a muzzle turned suddenly white, belabored breathing, a cough in the humid August heat (begun just hours before the last moment I saw her alive) and a complete loss of appetite since the week before, she unwaveringly maintained her youthful pursuit of her twenty-four-hour-a-day job: being my ears.

Leaning heavily on my cane, on my way to a New York City hospital for surgery, I said to our veterinarian, "... must be the heat—the breathing, the cough, the lack of interest in food." Sheena tugged at an attendant's leash pulling her away from me, doe-like eyes wide, ears straight up, her signal for distress: Don't leave me in my most unfavorite place!

I did not know she was dying.

There was no stir in my silence all that autumn of 1994, as I remembered her. Puppyish as she was, it was easy to forget her age. Keenly responsive to sound, she had been wandering the streets of New York, a one- or two-year-old orange bundle of energy eager for life, for hard work, when the Guide Dog Foundation for the Blind (Smithtown, New York) took her home, training her to listen for deaf ears.

It had only been a few years since the mid-1970s, when the American Humane Society in Colorado began the hearing dog program. Lost and abandoned dogs found in shelters were selected (often saving their lives) to alert the deaf and hard of hearing to sound, signals often important for a person's safety. Besides obedience training, hearing dogs report to their persons a knock on the door, the ring of a telephone, a smoke alarm, an alarm clock, the cry of a child, and so many other sound-touches of life taken for granted when we have hearing.

Working dogs become protective, devoted. During our first year together Sheena spent three weeks in the hospital, her recovery uncertain for days. She had thrown herself in front of a speeding pickup truck, pushing me aside when I did not pay attention to her urgent signals. The boatyard we lived in at the time had little parking space. My old jeep was partially out on a treacherous curve of the narrow shore road. Preoccupied while unloading my groceries, I did not notice the actions of my devoted dog or my boatyard friends running toward me.

The young man who hit her lifted my badly injured dog off the hood of his pickup, signaled for me to get in, driving us to our veterinarian, and hospitalization for Sheena.

Throughout her days with me, Sheena's hours were long, never routine, requiring quick thinking, sudden decisions. Twenty-four hours a day she enlarged the world for me, telling me the usual, the special happenings I might miss in the abstraction of writing, in the quiet of sleep, for even in slumber I would be awakened with important messages: raccoon is on the dock; red fox is foraging across the creek; Elijah, one of our young felines, is on deck with a half-alive bird. I came to value her intuitive perceptions, quickly conveyed to me in our special language, her instinct for the rightness or wrongness of any situation, unerring.

In the language used to describe one's personal advisor or confidante, she was not my right arm; she was my ears, trotting by my side, running the gauntlet of global sound, informing me of it and its relative importance to our lives. She took no vacations from her job, which lasted twelve years and five weeks. I was her whole life. No sound nuances of our lives—silences to me—were too little or too much for her.

We spent every minute of our lives together. Ironically, I was not with her when she died. I was recovering from hip surgery when my husband Harvey brought her to see me. At the door of the hospital she took her last breath. A mischievous, delicate creature found as a stray was given purpose in life by a training center looking for alert dogs to be trained for a profoundly wonderful endeavor: to be someone's ears.

The teakwood gate to our floating home remained open that autumn, heavy rain darkening its exotic Asian surface. No orange furry creature leaned near the opening, watching, always watching, always listening. Letters came to me: "It was a privilege to know her." "She remains a marvelous spirit in our memories, and by extension, for other guide dogs." "She taught me to listen to animals. We will always remember her unselfishness and how she rescued you from danger over and over again. What a brave animal she was!"

Early on October 19th, 1994, we sailed out of Glen Cove Creek, letting the wind decide our course, light whispering winds whiffling the waters, a round tin of ashes on my lap. Where? We knew.

Gliding home I sat on the bowsprit, her favorite perch, trailing through my fingers crumbly grey and orange bits of herself, tossing her lightly over the rail into the creek, towards the brush where red fox and cubs often emerge, leaving traces of her along the mud flats where the great blue herons and great egrets stalk and thousands of gulls sit facing into the wind.

I tossed her ashes in mid-creek where she watched cormorants diving for flounder, and along the current coursing under the *Bette Anne*, our first home. Harvey tossed fortune cookies we had been saving, her favorite food. I clipped all my begonia blossoms, the portulacas and cosmos hanging over the rail, the petunias on deck, the leafy top of an avocado plant. They floated on the narrow creek, a wispy blanket over lengthening shadows of late afternoon. She was alive at that moment—scattered on deck, on our clothes by a willful changing wind, part of me always—that alert intelligence, that decisive mind, that puckish, playful spirit that was the essence of my Sheena.

I reached into a pocket, pulling out a photograph of my future companion, training at that very moment to be my new ears. Young energy, a bubbling personality leaped from the picture, absorbing the ache of the moment, perchance imbued by a heritage, a mission thus bequeathed. Sheena's legacy.

~~~~~~~~~

The following December 2nd, Smudge, a stray retrieved from a Colorado shelter, flew to her new East Coast home with her trainers from International Hearing Dog, Inc. Martha Foss, Director of IHDI, began the training of hearing dogs with the American Humane Society more than twenty-five years ago. Smudge, romping, irrepressible, a superb listener, demonstrated her outstanding training every minute, watching winter ducks and diving kingfishers, a child awed by a new adventure, reporting every wonder and sound to me (then placing her nose on the cookie jar for her reward), a bouncing creature given life, purpose, a home—my new ears—stirring a too-long four-month silence, lying this moment across my toes.

*Smudge—the author's "new ears"*

# PART III
# ELEGY FOR SHEENA
*August 9, 1994*

*A south wind took you*
  *on zephyr-soft thermals ...*
    *no longer my ears trotting always by my side*
*Pigeons ride the thermals ... and one osprey, two hawks*
  *pigeons on the window ledge*
   *beside my hospital bed*
*waiting*
  *for your visit*
*A grey-edged morning sun*
  *I ask Harvey to hurry ...*
    *dog biscuits in my robe pocket ... waiting ...*
*at the door of the hospital nine floors below me*
  *you stop breathing*
*Zephyr-soft thermals ruffle your orange fur,*
*your remarkable ears ...*
   *in my room Harvey holds you*
    *my numb fingers caress you*
     *you are still warm ...*
*I reach for those ears that have been my ears ...*
  *leave tears on your rugged flank*
   *to be cremated with you ...*
*And I cannot say goodbye ....*

                   *Hannah Merker*
                   *Copyright 8/94*

*Sheena at the door to the pilot house of* Haimish
*just four months before her death.*

Hannah Merker—a writer, book reviewer, professor of English litera-
ture and creative writing, and the executive editor of *Academic Library
Book Review* during its 12-year life—lived aboard the Good Ship *Bette
Anne* on the shores of Long Island Sound for over 20 years, always
with a hearing guide dog and a constantly changing population of cats.
She was a reference librarian for over 30 years with various Long
Island, New York, libraries and the United States Merchant Marine
Academy. She also established and served as the director of a division
of the Library of Congress' program for the visually and physically
handicapped of Suffolk County, New York. Hannah now lives in
Bristol, Maine, with water-dog/hearing guide dog Smudge, four of her
boatyard cats (who still look for puddles every day—reminders of their
life at sea), and a new young tomcat, three-legged Hopper. She is
currently working on two books: *Waterborn* and *Harvey's Brain*.

# Acknowledgments

O ur inspirations have been our pets—those who came before—and now, Sweep, Murphy, and Suzy, who snuggled when we became discouraged and tolerated upheaval in our homes during our work on this book

Hazel's son Bill provided understanding, patience, and countless hours of computer help. Her son Charles, his wife Theresa, and their little daughters Shani, Liana, and Farin, brought joyful respite and renewed energy with every visit.

Jackie's husband John served as sounding board, insightful commentator, and provider of endless moral support.

The contributing authors made this book possible. Their love for their pets moved them to write these stories to help other less fortunate animals.

Periodic consultations with representatives of the CRARL Board of Directors set the parameters within which we proceeded. We acknowledge, especially, Bobbie Grant, Margaret Morey, Carolyn Marsh, Katie Heckel, Carol Achterhof, and CRARL attorney Carol Chen.

Marcia G. Corradini, Esq. guided us well in copyright and other legal matters.

Chris McLarty, of Silverline Studio, Camden, Maine, skillfully and artistically transformed manuscript (text and photos) into the final layout for the book.

Many others have helped bring this project to fruition. We happily bow to the following: John Hanson, Gretchen Piston Ogden, Thomas Albury, Ronald Dyer, Keith Munson, John McKay, John Higgins, Staci Veitch, Karin Womer, Jeremy Townsend, Terri Fyler, Tim McCreight, Jenny Hall, Michelle Roberts, Anne Bertus, Matthew Olsen, Timothy Whelan, Dianne Flemming, Sharon Carlee, Brian Hansen, Jean Hayes, and Laurel Milos.

And in those important circles of extended family and close friends, there were many who in large and small ways asked questions, offered suggestions, and reinforced our resolve at every step of the long journey into print.

We acknowledge everyone's support with sincere gratitude.

≋

Thanks, also, to photographer and designer Jim Dugan of Camden, Maine, who created our website: www.wetpetsbook.com. The site provides glimpses into the treasures awaiting readers of this collection and offers a direct link to Trafford Publishing for ordering online.

# *About the Editors*

## HAZEL H. WEIDMAN

Hazel H. Weidman, currently owned by a rescued street cat named Sweep, is a retired professor of social anthropology from the University of Miami in Florida. She received her B.Sc. from Northwestern University, her A.M. and Ph.D. degrees from Harvard University.

For many years Dr. Weidman was active in bringing medical anthropology into focus and structure within the framework of the American Anthropological Association. There is now a Society for Medical Anthropology, which is an affiliate of that parent body. She is well published in her field and founded the Medical Anthropology Newsletter, which has evolved into the *International Journal of Medical Anthropology*. She has taught at the College of William and Mary, the University of Alabama School of Medicine, and, for twenty-one years, at the University of Miami School of Medicine.

At the time of her retirement from the University of Miami in 1989 she was Professor of Social Anthropology and Director, Office of Transcultural Education and Research in the Department of Psychiatry at the medical school.

Hazel recently moved from her retirement home in Camden, Maine, to an active life care community in Scarborough, Maine, where her interests continue in support of the Camden-Rockport Animal Rescue League. For several years she served as a member of its Board of Directors.

# JACQUELINE K. TEARE

Jackie Teare, co-owned by two shelter cats—a feisty feline named Murphy and a sweet, scaredy cat named Suzy—is a freelance writer with more than thirty years of experience as writer and editor, in locations ranging from Washington D.C. to Guam.

A veteran of The Associated Press in Michigan, Newhouse News Service in Washington D.C., and a feature placement service in the Capitol area, her work has appeared in newspapers around the country. Her reporting has focused on a wide range of topics, from national politics to regional business, agriculture, and social services issues.

A native of Massachusetts, she received both a B.A. and an M.A. in journalism from Michigan State University. In the 1960s, she became the first woman in Michigan to accept an invitation to join the previously all-male Society of Professional Journalists (Sigma Delta Chi).

Jackie started the Camden-Rockport Animal Rescue League's current newsletter, The Pet Connection, in 1994 and has remained as its volunteer editor. She also served on the CRARL Board of Directors for several years. She lives in Rockport, Maine, with her husband, John.

# Give the Gift of
# *Wet Pets and Other Watery Tales*
## to your Family Members, Friends, and Colleagues

Check your local bookstore or order here
All proceeds are donated to charity in support of animal welfare

This book is available from Trafford Publishing
by mail, phone, fax, e-mail, or the Internet

### MAIL:

Trafford Publishing
Suite 6E, 2333 Government Street,
Victoria, BC, Canada V8T 4P4

### CALL TOLL-FREE:

1-888-232-4444 (Canada & US only)
9:00 AM – 3:00 PM Eastern Time

### SEND A FAX:

250-383-6840

### E-MAIL:

bookstore@trafford.com

### ORDER ONLINE:

www.trafford.com/robots/03-1894.html
ISBN 1-4120-1516-2

We thank you for your interest

## *Enjoy!*

ISBN 1412015162

9 781412 015165